SpringerBriefs in History of Computing

Series Editor

Gerard Alberts, Institute for Mathematics, University of Amsterdam Institute for Mathematics, Amsterdam, The Netherlands

Springer Briefs in History of Computing presents concise summaries which address the history of computing, with an emphasis on the 'externalist' view of this history, more accessible to a wider audience. The series examines content and history from four main quadrants: the history of relevant technologies, the history of the core science, the history of relevant business and economic developments, and the history of computing as it pertains to social history and societal developments.

The series provides a forum for shorter works which may not suit the traditional book model. SpringerBriefs are compact volumes of 50 to 125 pages; between the limit of a journal review article and a conventional book.

Typical topics might include:

- An overview or review of an important historical topic of broad interest
- Biographies of key scientists, entrepreneurs, and organizations
- New historical research of interest to the computer science community
- Historical documents such as letters, manuscripts, or reports, together with annotation and analysis
- Works addressing social aspects of computing history

Briefs allow authors to present their ideas and readers to absorb them with minimal time investment. Briefs are published as part of Springer's eBook collection, with millions of users worldwide. In addition, Briefs are available for individual print and electronic purchase. Briefs are characterized by fast, global electronic dissemination, standard publishing contracts, easy-to-use manuscript preparation and formatting guidelines, and expedited production schedules. Both solicited and unsolicited manuscripts are considered for publication in this series.

William Aspray · David Hemmendinger

The Making and Meanings of a Computing Reference Work

Exploring the *Encyclopedia of Computer Science*

William Aspray [iD]
Charles Babbage Institute
University of Minnesota Twin Cities
Minneapolis, MN, USA

David Hemmendinger
Department of Computer Science
Union College
Schenectady, NY, USA

ISSN 2662-3005   ISSN 2662-3013 (electronic)
SpringerBriefs in History of Computing
ISBN 978-3-032-07416-4   ISBN 978-3-032-07417-1 (eBook)
https://doi.org/10.1007/978-3-032-07417-1

© The Editor(s) (if applicable) and The Author(s), under exclusive license to Springer Nature Switzerland AG 2026

This work is subject to copyright. All rights are solely and exclusively licensed by the Publisher, whether the whole or part of the material is concerned, specifically the rights of translation, reprinting, reuse of illustrations, recitation, broadcasting, reproduction on microfilms or in any other physical way, and transmission or information storage and retrieval, electronic adaptation, computer software, or by similar or dissimilar methodology now known or hereafter developed.
The use of general descriptive names, registered names, trademarks, service marks, etc. in this publication does not imply, even in the absence of a specific statement, that such names are exempt from the relevant protective laws and regulations and therefore free for general use.
The publisher, the authors and the editors are safe to assume that the advice and information in this book are believed to be true and accurate at the date of publication. Neither the publisher nor the authors or the editors give a warranty, expressed or implied, with respect to the material contained herein or for any errors or omissions that may have been made. The publisher remains neutral with regard to jurisdictional claims in published maps and institutional affiliations.

This Springer imprint is published by the registered company Springer Nature Switzerland AG
The registered company address is: Gewerbestrasse 11, 6330 Cham, Switzerland

If disposing of this product, please recycle the paper.

Contents

1 **An Encyclopedia of Computer Science** 1
2 **Audience** 11
   2.1 Encyclopedia Scholars on Audience 11
   2.2 ECS Audience 15
3 **Stance and Style** 21
   3.1 Encyclopedia Scholars on Stance and Style 21
   3.2 ECS Stance and Style 24
4 **Content** 29
   4.1 Encyclopedia Scholars on Content 29
   4.2 ECS Content 32
5 **The Editorial Process** 37
   5.1 Encyclopedia Scholars on the Editorial Process 37
   5.2 ECS Editorial Process 43
6 **Funding and Publishing** 47
   6.1 Encyclopedia Scholars on Funding and Publishing 47
   6.2 ECS Funding and Publishing 49
7 **Editions, Supplements, and Online Encyclopedias** 53
   7.1 Encyclopedia Scholars on Editions, Supplements, and Online Encyclopedias 53
   7.2 ECS Editions, Supplements, and Online Versions 56
8 **Cultural Artifact** 63
   8.1 Encyclopedia Scholars on the Encyclopedia as a Cultural Artifact 63
   8.2 ECS as a Cultural Object 68
9 **An Intellectual Field and Its Reference Tools** 73

Bibliography 79

About the Authors

William Aspray is Senior Research Fellow with the Charles Babbage Institute at the University of Minnesota Twin Cities. He has formerly taught at Colorado (Boulder), Harvard, Indiana (Bloomington), Texas (Austin), and Williams in departments of mathematical sciences, history of science, or information studies. He has also held senior management positions at the Charles Babbage Institute, Computing Research Association, and the IEEE History Center. He has written on the history of computing and information, information policy, and everyday information behavior. Many years ago, he conducted an oral history interview with Anthony Ralston, the principal editor of the *Encyclopedia of Computer Science*.

David Hemmendinger is Associate Editor in Chief of the *IEEE Annals of the History of Computing* and has served as its Editor in Chief. He has taught at Antioch, CUNY, Kenyon, Ohio State, Union, and Wright State in divisions of humanities and in departments of philosophy and of computer science. He has written on philosophy, history of science, computer science, computing history, and computing education. He was Co-editor of the *Encyclopedia of Computer Science*, fourth edition, and has written over 20 articles for the *Encyclopaedia Britannica*.

Chapter 1
An Encyclopedia of Computer Science

Abstract This chapter provides a general introduction to encyclopedias and a dozen other reference works such as atlases, dictionaries, and chronologies. It also discusses the origins and ongoing development of the *Encyclopedia of Computer Science*.

> Indeed, the purpose of an encyclopedia is to collect knowledge disseminated around the globe; to set forth its general system to the men with whom we live, and transmit it to those who will come after us, so that the work of preceding centuries will not become useless to the centuries to come; and so that our offspring, becoming better instructed, will at the same time become more virtuous and happy, and that we should not die without having rendered a service to the human race in the future years to come.[1]

During the last quarter of the twentieth century, the *Encyclopedia of Computer Science* (ECS) was the go-to reference source in computer science. The principal editor of the encyclopedia, Anthony Ralston, and the editors of the *IEEE Annals of the History of Computing* recognized the importance of this book to the emerging computing profession; and as a result, twenty years ago, Ralston published an *Annals* article about his experiences with the encyclopedia.[2] The article briefly describes what led to his editing it and the steps he took to produce it: engaging an editorial board, writing a prospectus, deciding on its organization, finding authors, and then dunning them to obtain their articles if they were tardy. It continues on to describe the changes in subsequent editions, their timing and their sales, the multiple changes in publisher over the course of the four editions, and the prospects for a fifth edition in print or online.

---

[1] Denis Diderot and Jean le Rond d'Alembert. 1751–1772, as quoted in the Wikipedia article on Encyclopedia, accessed March 17, 2025.

[2] Ralston 2004.

© The Author(s), under exclusive license to Springer Nature Switzerland AG 2026
W. Aspray and D. Hemmendinger, *The Making and Meanings of a Computing Reference Work*, SpringerBriefs in History of Computing,
https://doi.org/10.1007/978-3-032-07417-1_1

Ralston wrote the article for an audience interested in the history of computer science and of computing more generally, and so he presented the story of the ECS as a moment in that history. Its context was the state of computing as a discipline and, secondarily, the vicissitudes of publishers and publishing. It mentions several possible competitors only in passing and as being different in scope from the ECS. More important, it does not place the ECS in the context of other encyclopedias, of related reference works, and of reference works as a marker of the maturity of an academic discipline or a profession. We address each of these issues in this study.

An encyclopedia is a complex information artifact, a single work created by the cooperative efforts of hundreds or thousands of people and used in many ways by various readers. To better understand the creation and place in society of the *Encyclopedia of Computer Science*, we have examined an extensive scholarly literature on the history and nature of encyclopedias generally and then used this literature to probe more deeply into the story of the ECS.[3] This study is organized as follows: It begins with some introductory material about the history of the ECS, as well as some material about other reference tools available for the study of computing and draws some conclusions at the end. In between there are seven sections on various aspects of an encyclopedia, using a call-and-response format—with calls from the general encyclopedia scholarly literature, followed by a response relating those issues to the ECS.

We adopt this approach rather than simply interviewing the various people principally involved in editing or overseeing this encyclopedia. Unfortunately, most of them are not available to talk with. To help other scholars interested in computing history or encyclopedia history with their investigations, we have adopted an unorthodox practice of including not only our analysis of ECS but also questions we would have liked to address but did not have sources of answers.

To a certain degree, this encyclopedia marks a singular time in the history of encyclopedias concerning computer science. While there have been several computer science encyclopedias published since then (see Table 1.2), the ability to search for information about computer science online has reduced the value of encyclopedias to computing professionals and the general public alike.

---

[3] We have quoted many of the books on the history and nature of encyclopedias in future chapters. In addition to those texts, the following publications provide useful background on this topic: Chamberlain 2023, Donato 1993, Eliade 1973, Geiger and Anderson 2017, Loveland and Reagle 2019, Stecchini 1962, Stover 1962, Todorovic 2018, and Yeo 2001 and 2007. The *Encyclopaedia Britannica* plays a special role in this history; see Auchter 1999, Danowitz 2017, Gronas et al. 2012, Kruse 1958, and Messner and DiStaso 2013. Our main interest is in encyclopedias about computing and computer science, but there has been reflection on the making of an encyclopedia of the related field of library and information science (Bates and Maack 2009; Bates 2007 and 2010).

This study identifies many of the issues that would be addressed in conceiving, writing, editing, publishing, and revising an encyclopedia generally; and this analysis is then used to probe more deeply than Ralston does in his *Annals* article the creation and distribution of this particular encyclopedia. One of us (Hemmendinger) was a coeditor of the final edition of this encyclopedia; the other of us (Aspray) had previously conducted an oral history with Ralston and has written extensively on computing history. Understanding this key reference source is a way to better understand the history of computing as an academic discipline and as a profession.

About the *Encyclopedia of Computer Science*

The *Encyclopedia of Computer Science* was published in four editions between 1976 and 2000. It was initially edited solely by Anthony Ralston, who continued to coedit the following editions, and was probably the first one-volume encyclopedia on the subject. Ralston describes its origin in the *Annals* article: in 1971. Isaac Auerbach, a computing entrepreneur and publisher, suggested it; and Ralston thought that the discipline had become well-enough established for there to be a comprehensive reference book on it.

Ralston had a mathematics Ph.D. and had taught mathematics at Stevens Institute of Technology, where he also ran its computer center. (As computer science degree programs were quite new, most people who worked in the field had come to it from mathematics or engineering; and many had worked in computing centers prior to the creation of computer science departments.) While at Stevens, Ralston wrote books on mathematics for digital computing (1962)[4] and on numerical analysis (1965),[5] and he remained interested in the mathematics of computing and in mathematics education. In 1965 he became the computer center director at the State University of New York at Buffalo, and in 1967, the founding head of its computer science department.[6] He was active in the Association of Computing Machinery (ACM), one of the principal professional organizations for computing; he was its Vice President, 1970–72, and President, 1972–74. During 1975–76 he was president of the American Federation of Information Processing Societies (AFIPS).

Ralston's roles in the professional societies put him in contact with many of the leading figures in computer science, a much smaller field fifty years ago—he remarked in an interview,[7] "I effectively knew everyone." He was able to recruit a number of these contacts to serve as authors or recommend other potential authors. The ECS also had an editorial board to help plan the list of articles as well as to recommend authors. In a prospectus, Ralston wrote that the goals of the ECS were:

---

[4] Ralston and Wilf 1962.

[5] Ralston 1965.

[6] Anthony Ralston interview, Interviewers William Aspray and Bernard de Neumann, ACM Oral Histories no. 6, January 10, 2006. https://doi.org/10.1145/1141880.1147774.

[7] Ralston interview, p. 7.

1. To provide a comprehensive basic reference to the subject matter of computer science, and
2. To provide a broad picture of computer science through survey and essay articles on a considerable number of subjects.[8]

The organization of computer science into ten areas that the ECS introduced became the basis of the taxonomy of the field used by the American Federation of Information Processing Societies.

The first edition of the ECS contained 470 articles in 1523 pages and cost $60. It received favorable reviews in the ACM *Computers and Society* magazine[9] and in *Datamation*.[10] After several years, Ralston began to edit a second edition, this time with Edwin Reilly of the State University at Albany as associate editor. It appeared in 1983, and added "*and Engineering*" to the title, although that was dropped for the final two editions. The second edition grew to 550 articles and 1664 pages, priced at $87.50. It was adopted by the book club Library of Computer and Information Science, which made it a subscriber introductory offer, selling about 100,000 copies.

The third edition, with Reilly as full coeditor, was published in 1993, with 605 articles in slightly fewer though larger pages and sold for $100. The fourth and final edition, with David Hemmendinger as a coeditor together with Ralston and Reilly, grew significantly to 2034 pages with 623 articles. It cost $150 when published, slightly less than the first edition after taking inflation into account, although the price soon rose to $200. While the first three editions sold about 11,000–12,000 copies, excluding the book club sales, the fourth edition sold only half as many by 2004. We will discuss possible reasons for that drop-off in sales later, as well as the reasons for there not having been a fifth edition; a major factor was probably the rise of online search and reference tools such as Wikipedia, which began shortly after the fourth edition appeared.

About Encyclopedias and Other Reference Tools

The encyclopedia is a type of reference tool that provides overview information on a particular topic. While there are general encyclopedias intended to cover all of knowledge for a general audience—such as *Encyclopaedia Britannica*, which we discuss in passing—the main concern here is with specialized encyclopedias that are intended to cover the complete knowledge of a particular academic profession or discipline. The oldest encyclopedias are about 2000 years old, notably *Naturalis Historia* compiled by Pliny the Elder in the first century AD. The most famous encyclopedia was the one created by Denis Diderot and Jean le Rond d'Alembert in the eighteenth century— quoted in the epigraph above—for it was a principal embodiment of the notion of enlightenment thought. While there is a long history of specialized encyclopedias, they really came into their own beginning in the late nineteenth century with the creation of new academically oriented professions involving science, engineering, the humanities, and the social sciences to complement traditional professions such as

---

[8] Quoted in Ralston 2004, p. 42.
[9] Landis 1976.
[10] Granholm 1976.

medicine and law and accelerating in pace after the Second World War. When a body of knowledge became coherent and was associated with a new branch of academic study and a new occupation with its own professional standards, there was then a place for an encyclopedia of this specialized discipline.

While computing also goes back to antiquity, rapid advances in computing theory and practices were stimulated by the Second World War. New professional societies for computing were formed in the 1950s, the first academic departments were created in the 1960s, and the general application of computing to societal problems beyond military applications became familiar in the 1970s. Thus, by the last quarter of the twentieth century, the computing field was ripe for a specialized encyclopedia; and the *Encyclopedia of Computer Science* served that function admirably through four editions in that quarter century.

Encyclopedias are but one of a dozen or more types of reference tools. Table 1.1 lists many of them, describes briefly the purpose of each, and gives some examples.

Table. 1.1 Reference tools[11]

Reference tool	Purpose	Examples
Encyclopedias	Summaries of knowledge in a particular discipline	**Encyclopedia of Computer Science**, Encyclopaedia Britannica, Stanford Encyclopedia of Philosophy
Dictionaries	Alphabetic list of words in one language with their definitions and usage	**Oxford Dictionary of Computer Science**, Merriam Webster Dictionary, Black's Law Dictionary
Biographical dictionaries	An organized collection of biographies of individuals that fall into a particular class	**International Biographical Dictionary of Computer Pioneers (John A.N. Lee),** Dictionary of American Biography, Dictionary of Scientific Biography
Handbooks/ manuals/guides	Detailed information about a specific subject for specialists	**Computer Science Handbook (Allen B. Tucker),** Zappo's Culture Handbook, Maynard's Industrial Engineering Handbook

(continued)

---

[11] Modified definitions based on a Google search of "what are the 14 types of reference materials?"

Table. 1.1 (continued)

Reference tool	Purpose	Examples
Almanacs	A regularly published listing of a set of current information about one or multiple subjects	**Computer Industry Almanac**, The Farmer's Almanac, TIME Almanac with Information Please
Directories	Organized list of people and/or organizations, together with contact information	**ACM Staff Directory**, Yellow Pages, Best of the Web
Atlases	A collection of maps presenting political, cultural, physical, road, or other information	**The Atlas of Cyberspace**,[12] Rand McNally Road Atlas, North American Environmental Atlas
Indexes	Compilations on information, generally arranged either alphabetically or numerically, that indicate the location of related information	**Archives of Data Processing History: A Guide of Major United States' Collections (James. W. Cortada)**, Index Librorum Prohibitorum, Federal Register
Bibliographies	Comprehensive lists of resources that share one or more common attributes about a particular topic	**A Bibliographic Guide to the History of Computer Applications, 1950–1990 (James W. Cortada)**, International Bibliography of the Social Sciences, The Martin Gardner Bibliography (Dana Richards and Donald Knuth)
Thesaurus (synonym dictionary)	Lists of synonyms and antonyms of words	**Barnes & Noble Thesaurus of Computer Science**, Roget's Thesaurus, The Clinician's Thesaurus
Yearbooks	An annual publication providing events, statistics, or other information about a particular year	**Namibia University Yearbook 2023, Faculty of Computing and Informatics**, 1935 US Yearbook, The Wrestling Yearbook 2024

(continued)

---

[12] Martin Dodge ran the Cybergeography Research project from 1997 to 2004, the geographical portion of his efforts is at the "Geographic" link on his inactive web page at https://personalpages.manchester.ac.uk/staff/m.dodge/cybergeography/atlas/atlas.html (accessed 28 April 2025). See also Kitchin and Dodge 2002, which can be downloaded at https://kitchin.org/atlas/.

Dominic Walliman created a so-called Map of Computer Science for the Data Visualization Society's Information is Beautiful Awards. See https://www.informationisbeautifulawards.com/showcase/2333-map-of-computer-science (accessed 28 April 2025). This is an intellectual mapping rather than a geographical mapping.

Perhaps some of the studies of geography and computing include maps of computing in the sense we mean. See Downey 2024 for an overview of the literature on geography in the history of computing.

Table. 1.1 (continued)

Reference tool	Purpose	Examples
Gazeteers (geographical dictionary)	Brief descriptive, geographical, historical, and statistical information on specific places	**The Digital Flood: The Diffusion of Information Technology Across the U.S., Europe, and Asia (James W. Cortada)**, Merriam-Webster's Geographical Dictionary, Historical and Geographical Dictionary of Japan (Edmond Papinot)
Chronologies (timelines)	Summaries of the advancement of an event or field by supplying brief milestones in the progression through time	**Timeline of Computer History (Computer History Museum),** The People's Chronology: A Year-by-year Record of Human Events from Prehistory to the Present (James Trager), A Chronology of Film: A Cultural Timeline from the Magic Lantern to Netflix ((Ian Hadyn Smith)
Statistical collections and specialized training	Statistical information on organized topics	**Probability and Statistics for Computer Science (Michael Baron)**, Statistical Tables and Formulae: A Collection of Tables and Formulas in Statistics and Probability (Kingsley Augustine), CRC Basic Statistical Tables (William H. Beyer)
Mathematical collections and specialized tables	Information about mathematical functions and formulas	**Mathematics for Computer Scientists (Peter Hartmann),** Mathematical Formulas for Economists (Bernd Luderer et al.), CRC Standard Mathematical Tables and Formulas (Daniel Zwillinger)
Reference management tools	Software to organize, store, and manage references	Endnote, Mendeley, Zotero, Citavi, PaperPile

The examples in boldface are ones specifically concerned with computing. This table offers only a small number of examples of each of these types of reference tool, while Table 1.2 provides a more extensive (but not exhaustive) list of English-language encyclopedias about computing and closely related topics.

Table. 1.2 Encyclopedias of computer science and closely related disciplines[13]

Adam, F., & Humphreys, P. (Eds.). (2008). *Encyclopedia of Decision Making and Decision Support Technologies* (Vol. 2). IGI Global

Adamatzky, A. (2018). *Cellular Automata: A Volume in the Encyclopedia of Complexity and Systems Science.* Springer

Alhajj, R., & Rokne, J. (2014). *Encyclopedia of Social Network Analysis and Mining.* Springer

Ang, M. H., Khatib, O., & Siciliano, B. (Eds.). (2019). *Encyclopedia of Robotics.* Springer

Baillieul, J., & Samad, T. (Eds.). (2021). *Encyclopedia of Systems and Control.* Springer

Belzer, J, Holzman, A.G., Kent, A, 1975 (1993). *Encyclopedia of Computer Science and Technology.* **Marcel Dekker. (Many specialized volumes)**

Ben-Menahem, A. (2009). *Historical Encyclopedia of Natural and Mathematical Sciences.* Springer

Besançon, R. (2013). *The Encyclopedia of Physics.* Springer

Cartelli, A., & Palma, M. (Eds.). (2008). *Encyclopedia of Information Communication Technology.* IGI Global

Comandé, G. (Ed.). (2022). *Elgar Encyclopedia of Law and Data Science.* Edward Elgar Publishing

Considine, D. M., & Considine, G. D. (2013). *Van Nostrand's Scientific Encyclopedia.* Springer

Dodge, Y. (2008). *The Concise Encyclopedia of Statistics.* Springer

Engquist, B. (Ed.). (2015). *Encyclopedia of Applied and Computational Mathematics.* Springer

Feather, J., & Sturges, P. (2003). *International Encyclopedia of Information and Library Science.* Routledge

Floudas, C. A., & Pardalos, P. M. (Eds.). (2008). *Encyclopedia of Optimization.* Springer

François, C. (Ed.). (2004). *International Encyclopedia of Systems and Cybernetics.* De Gruyter Saur

Françoise, J. P., Naber, G. L., & Tsou, S. T. (Eds.). (2004). *Encyclopedia of Mathematical Physics.* Oxford, UK: Elsevier

Freire, M., & Pereira, M. (Eds.). (2007). *Encyclopedia of Internet Technologies and Applications.* IGI Global

Furht, B. (Ed.). (2008). *Encyclopedia of Multimedia.* Springer

Gass, S. I., & Harris, C. M. (1996). *Encyclopedia of Operations Research and Management Science.* Kluwer

Gellert, W. (Ed.). (2012). *The VNR Concise Encyclopedia of Mathematics.* Springer

Ghaoui, C. (Ed.). (2005). *Encyclopedia of Human Computer Interaction.* **IGI global**

Gibson, J. D. (Ed.). (2012). *Mobile Communications Handbook.* CRC Press

Hempstead, C., & Worthington, W. (2005). *Encyclopedia of 20th-century Technology.* Routledge

Henderson, H. (2009). *Encyclopedia of Computer Science and Technology.* **Infobase Publishing**

Itō, K. (Ed.). (1993). *Encyclopedic Dictionary of Mathematics* (Vol. 1). MIT Press

Jones, S. (Ed.). (2002). *Encyclopedia of New Media: An Essential Reference to Communication and Technology.* Sage Publications

Kajan, E. (2001). *The Acronyms of Computer Science and Communications: A Comprehensive Acronym Dictionary and Illustrated Encyclopedia.* Springer

Katz, S., Reed, C. B., Balakrishnan, N. V., and Bidakovic, B. (2nd, ed., 2005). *Encyclopedia of Statistical Sciences.* John Wiley & Sons,

Kao, M. Y. (Ed.). (2008). *Encyclopedia of Algorithms.* Springer

Kent, A. K., Williams, J. G., Kent, R. (1988). *Encyclopedia of Microcomputers* **(Vol. 1). Marcel Dekker**

Khosrow-Pour, D. B. A. (Ed.). (2005). *Encyclopedia of Information Science and Technology.* IGI Global

Khosrow-Pour, D. B. A. (Ed.). (2020). *Encyclopedia of Organizational Knowledge, Administration, and Technology.* IGI Global

Kotz, S., Balakrishnan, N., Read, C. B., Vidakovic, B., & Johnson, N. L. (2005). *Encyclopedia of Statistical Sciences, Volume 1.* John Wiley & Sons

(continued)

---

[13] In addition to the encyclopedias listed here, we found approximately 25 publications listed as handbooks and not included here.

Table. 1.2 (continued)

LaPlante, P. A. (Ed.) (2016) *Encyclopedia of Computer Science and Technology*, Second Edition. CRC Press
Laplante, P. A. (Ed.). (2018). *Encyclopedia of Image Processing*. CRC Press
Laplante, P. A., Werghi, N., Kuszmavl, et al. (2017). *Dictionary of Computer Science, Engineering and Technology*. **CRC Press**
Lerman, S. (Ed.). (2020). *Encyclopedia of Mathematics Education*. Springer
Li, S. Z. (2009). *Encyclopedia of Biometrics: I-Z* (Vol. 1). Springer
Maimon, O., & Rokach, L. (Eds.). (2005). *Data Mining and Knowledge Discovery Handbook* (Vol. 2, No. 2005). Springer
Mattingly, J. (Ed.). (2022). *The SAGE Encyclopedia of Theory in Science, Technology, Engineering, and Mathematics*. SAGE Publications
McDonald, J. D., & Levine-Clark, M. (Eds.). (2017). *Encyclopedia of Library and Information Sciences*. CRC Press
Meyers, R. A. (Ed.). (2009). *Encyclopedia of Complexity and Systems Science* (Vol. 9). Springer
Padua, D. (Ed.). (2011). *Encyclopedia of Parallel Computing*. **Springer**
Paragios, N., Chen, Y., & Faugeras, O. D. (Eds.). (2006). *Handbook of Mathematical Models in Computer Vision*. Springer
Parker, S. P. (Ed.). (1988). *McGraw-Hill Encyclopedia of Electronics and Computers*. McGraw-Hill
Rabuñal, J. R., Dorado De La Calle, J., & Pazos Sierra, A. (Eds.). (2008). Encyclopedia of Artificial Intelligence. IGI Global
Ralston, A. (Ed.) (1976). *Encyclopedia of Computer Science*, 1st edition, Petrocelli/Charter
Ranganathan, S., Nakai, K., & Schonbach, C. (2018). *Encyclopedia of Bioinformatics and Computational Biology: ABC of Bioinformatics*. Elsevier
Rivero, L. C., Doorn, J. H., & Ferraggine, V. E. (Eds.). (2005). *Encyclopedia of Database Technologies andAapplications*. IGI Global
Rogers, P. L., Berg, G. A., Boettcher, J. V., Howard, C., Justice, L., & Schenk, K. D. (Eds.). (2009). *Encyclopedia of Distance Learning*. IGI Global
Rojas, R. (Ed.) (2001) *Encyclopedia of Computers and Computer History*, **Routledge**
Sakr, S., & Zomaya, A. Y. (Eds.). (2019). *Encyclopedia of Big Data Technologies*. Springer International Publishing
Sammut, C., & Webb, G. I. (Eds.). (2011). *Encyclopedia of Machine Learning*. Springer Science & Business Media
Schwarz, J. A., Contescu, C. I., & Putyera, K. (Eds.). (2004). *Dekker Encyclopedia of Nanoscience and Nanotechnology* (Vol. 5). CRC Press
Scott, A. (2006). *Encyclopedia of Nonlinear Science*. Routledge
Shapiro, L. R., & Maras, M. H. (Eds.). (2021). *Encyclopedia of Security and Emergency Management*. Springer
Shekhar, S., & Xiong, H. (Eds.). (2007). *Encyclopedia of GIS*. Springer Science & Business Media
Splinter, R. (2017). *Illustrated Encyclopedia of Applied and Engineering Physics*. CRC Press
Tanton, J. S. (2005). *Encyclopedia of Mathematics*. Infobase Publishing
Tatnall, A. (Ed.). (2020). *Encyclopedia of Education and Information Technologies*. Springer International Publishing
Trauth, E. M. (Ed.). (2006). *Encyclopedia of Gender and Information Technology*. IGI Global
Wah, B. W. (Ed.) (2007). *Wiley Encyclopedia of Computer Science and Engineering*. **Wiley-interscience**
Wang, J. (Ed.). (2023). *Encyclopedia of Data Science and Machine Learning*. IGI Global
Webster, J. J. 1999. *Wiley Encyclopedia of Electrical and Electronics Engineering*. John Wiley & Sons
Wieisstein, E. W.. (1998). *CRC Concise Encyclopedia of Mathematics,* Chapman & Hall/CRC
Wilson, R. A., & Keil, F. C. (Eds.). (2001). *The MIT Encyclopedia of the Cognitive Sciences (MITECS)*. MIT Press

Chapter 2
Audience

Abstract This chapter discusses issues of audience in writing an encyclopedia generally and in particular for the *Encyclopedia of Computer Science*. Topics include determining the audience(s), reaching multiple audiences, addressing readers who want to make practical use beyond basic knowledge, using accessible language, and anticipating potential future audiences.

2.1 Encyclopedia Scholars on Audience

One of the most important decisions to make in the production of an encyclopedia of computer science is to determine the audience. In the eighteenth and nineteenth centuries, encyclopedias were intended for the social elite. Encyclopedias then were published in expensive folio editions, with liberal use of Latin text, which was only accessible by the highly educated. Efforts in those centuries to make encyclopedias more accessible were criticized in some circles as contributing to the "vulgarization of knowledge."[1]

It was only in the twentieth century that there came to be a democratization of encyclopedias—a source of information for the "average [hu]man." But even in the first decades of the twentieth century, encyclopedias were not for everyone, as this quotation from encyclopedia historian Charles Van Doren indicates, but instead for educated professionals who strived for a wider understanding of their world:

> Who is the average man?...he is 'judge, lawyer, doctor, businessman, technician, or administrator'...who carries about with him the weight of an unsatisfied desire to understand the civilization in the eddies of which he flounders, without being able to rise himself high enough to see its total form.[2]

But it was not until after the Second World War, when servicemen were returning from the war, entering college in large numbers, and starting families, that the encyclopedia first was intended for a wider American public. The American publisher

---

[1] France 1998. On the challenges of multiple audiences, also see Menagarishvili 2012.
[2] Van Doren 1962, p. 26.

Funk & Wagnalls is a good example of this trend. It published its first "Standard Dictionary" in the 1890s and its first "Standard Encyclopedia" in 1912, but it really came into the American consciousness in 1953, when it was sold in supermarkets—99 cents for the first volume and $2.99 for subsequent volumes. For example, Dick Martin would often close a skit on his popular television show of the late 1960s, *Laugh In*, with the line "You can look that up in your Funk & Wagnalls!"[3]

Academic specialization began in the last quarter of the nineteenth century and grew rapidly after the Second World War. With this academic specialization came more specialized encyclopedias focused on a single academic discipline but intended for all people interested in the discipline (faculty members, students, working professionals, and interested members of the educated general public), as well as handbooks meant for practitioners and advanced students.[4]

Academic disciplines are not all alike. Nuclear engineering or mortuary science, for example, mostly attracts people who are studying or practicing that discipline. However, an encyclopedia of computer science—or one of computing, more generally—might attract a wider audience, including people with no formal training in the academic discipline, because of the great employment or hobbyist opportunities that computer science affords, because of curiosity, or because computing has become a support tool to a wide array of academic disciplines and professions. So, the readers of an encyclopedia may be quite diverse, making the preparation of an encyclopedia accessible to its many audiences more challenging.

The literature on the history of encyclopedias raises several important questions about language, tone, technical level of article, and comprehensiveness of coverage. While publication in English is usual for a computer science text, the general public in other countries (if not the professional community) may have difficulties reading English.[5] But even a reader who is fluent in English may be challenged if the conceptual or technical level of the writing is elevated. The goal of one social science encyclopedia, for example, was that "at least the basic information on all important topics would be accessible to the undergraduate student and the educated layman."[6] Having

---

[3] Funk & Wagnalls, Wikipedia, accessed December 10, 2024. When Microsoft created its first online encyclopedia in 1993, it failed to obtain rights to use the content from *Encyclopaedia Britannica* or *World Book Encyclopedia*, so it licensed access to the content from Funk & Wagnalls until it could create its own content.

The encyclopedia scholar Peter France 1998, p. 69, described how the people buying the various volumes of the encyclopedia might feel as though they were participating more actively in the educational process: "The subscriber associated with the enterprise in the manner of a shareholder." …"Such an association, or even the buying of a set of encyclopedias could flatter the reader with the impression of collaborating in a common cause."

[4] Encyclopedia scholar Tilottama Rajan 2007, p. 335, discusses the similarity between encyclopedias and universities in "how we construct disciplinarity and interdisciplinarity": "encyclopedias share something with universities, which also try to accommodate a multiplicity of knowledges, while organising them into disciplines and faculties that raise questions of what qualifies as knowledge, and where it is centred."

[5] See, for example, Kallman 1994 on the difficulties, for both authors and readers, of publishing in 1981 the *Encyclopedia of Music in Canada*.

[6] Sutton 1962, p. 28.

2.1 Encyclopedia Scholars on Audience

widely comprehensible articles may be a challenge for the author, who is most likely chosen for her technical knowledge, not for her facility with popular communication. As the well-known intellectual historian Jacques Barzun wrote:

> [The author] must make [the expert and the general reader] learn a common language in the very act of obtaining answers to their questions. This may occasionally be beyond the reach of his art, but an encyclopedia cannot be expected invariably to furnish its reader with matter that they can recognize in the language they already speak.[7]

In fact, one encyclopedia historian has criticized—in colorful language—the dry academic tone found in many encyclopedias:

> The tone of American encyclopedias is often fiercely inhuman. It appears to be the wish of some contributors to write about living institutions as if they were pickled frogs, outstretched upon a dissecting board. Most encyclopedias are seldom amusing or easy reading. Their tone is "academic" and "scientific"—no compromises are made with ignorance, and one has the feeling that contributors expect readers to be almost as learned, dull and unenthusiastic as themselves?[8]

In addition to writing in language that is accessible to a variety of communities, the encyclopedia editor must make guesses about who will want to read this work and what they will want to get out of it. The editors of a Canadian music encyclopedia were surprised by the large number of different groups interested in their book: musical performers; arts councils; national organizations of composers, educators, librarians, publishers, and recording companies; immigrant groups who brought their music to Canada, and others.[9] But how was the encyclopedia article writer or editor to know what each of these groups wanted to learn from their book? As one encyclopedia historian explained this point:

> An encyclopedia is essentially a reference work; the needs of readers should therefore be paramount in determining its scope and contents. This directive, however, is difficult to use as a basis for making decisions, since a wide range or reader sophistication and motivations must be considered.[10]

The editors of *The Encyclopedia of the Social Sciences* discussed how difficult it was for them to judge the audience for their new work:

> Our awareness that the encyclopedia would have to create its own demand led to a number of editorial decisions. An early concern was to try to gauge the audience. Little is known about who uses what kind of encyclopedias for what purposes. Our typical users, we guessed half jokingly, would be "the American graduate student and the assistant professor at the University of Bombay"—the first because of his need to pass his subject matter doctoral examination and the second because of his limited access to current American and European books and journals. We also guessed that some undergraduates would use the encyclopedia, and that mature students would use it to explore alien disciplines.[11]

---

[7] Barzun 1962, pp. 7–8.
[8] Van Doren 1962, p. 25.
[9] Kallman 1994, pp. 3–4.
[10] Sills 1962, p. 31.
[11] Sills 1969, p. 1174.

This issue is compounded by varying goals of the editors and authors of an encyclopedia. As the encyclopedia historian Peter France notes, encyclopedists "have different aims, which in a given publication can combine in varying proportions. For some the encyclopedia is a kind of home university in which they can resolutely pursue a course of instruction, ... Others seek the excitement of the new."[12]

Another way to consider the challenges of encyclopedia writing is to consider particular audiences in turn. First consider students and public education. One problematic temptation here is to write articles to the lowest common denominator, which is not helpful to the aspiring student who wants to grow—or to many other audiences.[13] As Barzun pithily explains this difficulty, how is the encyclopedist to "retain the respect of the experts [but write]…articles… useful to children and intelligible to their parents."[14]

The reference librarian Rachel Wexelbaum has pointed out an issue faced by the print encyclopedia. Once they are published, printed encyclopedias cannot be readily changed. As educational points of view change, with new interpretations of geography, history, politics, and LGBTQ and minority groups, the print encyclopedia is locked into an earlier perspective counter to current educational thinking. While this might be less of an issue with computer science material, it still exists for example with topics concerning the underrepresentation of various groups within computing, computing as a technology of colonization, or the social construction of technology as opposed to technological determinism.[15]

Libraries historically have been fans of encyclopedias.[16] As Wexelbaum elaborated:

> Before the internet, academic libraries purchased multivolume general encyclopedias. These encyclopedias were shelved in the reference area, often in close proximity to the reference desk. The librarian would receive a reference question, and might direct the patron to those encyclopedias. Academic libraries invested hundreds of thousands of dollars in print encyclopedias, and would have to purchase the latest editions to stay current. If the encyclopedia publishers spotted errors after publication, they would send out errata pages to librarians, who would cut and paste "correct" information over the old. Not all libraries followed this practice; less affluent libraries did not regularly update their encyclopedias.[17]

But with the coming of the Internet, this enthusiasm among reference librarians has somewhat faded:

> Wikipedia has caused academic librarians to question the value of traditionally published encyclopedias as a ready reference source. Many academic libraries weeding their print encyclopedia collections either replace them with reference subscriptions or not at all. Not

---

[12] France 1998, p. 68.

[13] See Couch 1962, p. 21.

[14] Barzun 1962, p. 7. Ashmore 1962, p. 15, more wordily makes this same point about checks and balances between academic and popular audiences.

[15] Wexelbaum 2012, p. 8. On the educational value of encyclopedias, also see Fenske 2010, p. 53; Menagarishvili 2012, Chap. 1.

[16] Sutton 1962, p. 27.

[17] Wexelbaum 2012, p. 8.

all academic librarians, however, believe that all encyclopedias should go the way of the used book sale. Encyclopedias addressing different cultures, religions, women, disabilities, LGBTIQ Studies, race and ethnicity, historical eras, philosophies, or subjects of local interest are often kept in the reference collection as examples of diverse viewpoints and cultural representatives. This is especially the case if the encyclopedia editors and contributors are renowned specialists in their fields. Encyclopedias produced during particular historical eras or cultural movements may also be retained as evidence of what scholars promoted as "fact" during that time.[18]

There is also a counterview of the value of the encyclopedia as a reference tool:

> American alphabetical encyclopedias at present leave much to be desired as reference works. For subjects of no great importance, which can be covered in short articles, they are admirable. In general, however, the more extensive the treatment (and hence the more important the subject), the more difficult it is to use modern encyclopedia articles for reference purposes.[19]

The encyclopedia historian Harry Ashmore has also noted two different uses by experts, which need to be taken into consideration when creating an encyclopedia: "A brain surgeon will not look up the article on brain surgery in order to prepare for a prefrontal lobotomy. But if he has access to the set he will turn to the articles out of natural curiosity—and on the basis of his own expert knowledge he will form his judgment as to the quality of the remainder."[20] Encyclopedia-like articles for experts in their specialty are more likely to be offered in handbooks rather than encyclopedias. These handbooks can be written at a higher level of technical detail, addressing the needs of smaller, more advanced audience. They are intended to help with advanced practice in a specialized technical area.

2.2 ECS Audience

Robert McHenry, editor in chief of the *Encyclopaedia Britannica*, 1992–1997,[21] said, "The dirty little secret of the encyclopedia industry is that we don't know whether or not people read what we publish."[22] Jeff Loveland, the author of a book on the history of encyclopedias,[23] cites McHenry's remark in a chapter on encyclopedia readers. It describes several categories of readers and users: those who have it on their shelves for adornment or learning through osmosis; those who acquire it for their children, for education or simply elevated seating; those who look to it for casual entertainment and for more systematic learning; and those who treat the updates to multivolume encyclopedias as a kind of periodical.

---

[18] Wexelbaum 2012, p. 9.

[19] Van Doren 1962, p. 25.

[20] Ashmore 1962, p. 15.

[21] According to https://www.britannica.com/biography/Robert-McHenry, accessed April 14, 2025. The reader who attends to these notes will have observed that our identification of McHenry draws on an online encyclopedia. We have more to say about such Web sites later.

[22] Robert McHenry, quoted in Rossney 1995, p. 80.

[23] Loveland 2019.

Where does the ECS stand among these uses? It was not a multivolume book and did not have annual updates. Although it may have been used to raise children's seating at a time when city telephone books were becoming scarce, we have no information about such use. The information that we do have about its use is largely indirect. We described the sales of the ECS editions in Chap. 1. Ralston commented that the second edition appeared in 1983, when scientific book clubs were popular. That date also roughly coincides with the introduction of the IBM PC at a time when personal computing was becoming better-known; that may also have stimulated interest in computing and influenced the choice of the ECS by the Library of Computer and Information Science.

The plans for the first edition of the ECS began in 1971, according to its editor, Anthony Ralston.[24] Computer science was still a new field, though he thought it ready for systematic treatment. In fact, the term, "computer science" is something of a misnomer both with regard to the subject matter and to the scope of the ECS. The term commonly denotes more than strictly scientific aspects and includes system design issues that might better be called "engineering" as well as numerous applications of computing to other disciplines. "Computing" might be a better term, or "informatics", which is often used in European countries. Nevertheless, we seem to be stuck with "computer science."

The first ECS edition had ten article categories, three of which were largely nontechnical: "Management, societal, economic, and legal aspects," "Professional and educational aspects," and "History". Its "Application" category also included nontechnical areas such as arts, humanities, and games. Although this classification changed a little in the subsequent editions, the balance of material did not change much, apart from accommodating the increased number of fields to which computing was applied. We discuss this further in Chap. 3.

The ECS had a distinctly Western focus, perhaps not surprisingly, as much of the computer science work was done in the United States or Western Europe. Its coverage of work in the United Kingdom was quite extensive, with some attention to continental Europe, e.g., to Konrad Zuse's computers in Germany and programming language research in France and Switzerland. Even the fourth edition had nothing on early Soviet computers, although mathematical work received some attention. The article on computer science education addressed the curricular standards of the Association of Computing Machinery, a major international computing organization, and had sections on education in Europe and in Asia as well as (primarily) in the United States.

The ECS preface describes the book as a snapshot ("[which] is what an encyclopedia is"), and Ralston wrote that although some of it would become outdated in a half-decade or more, much would remain valuable well after that. Its foreword describes it as intended for "the layman or the nonspecialist who needs elaboration on a subject in which he is not expert," and that it attempts to be comprehensive in breadth though necessarily not in depth. Subsequent editions revised this characterization to:

---

[24] Ralston 2004.

2.2 ECS Audience

> The most important purpose of an encyclopedia in a particular discipline is to be a basic reference work for readers who need information on subjects in which they are not expert.[25]

(The second edition preface adds that it has eliminated the use of masculine pronouns that do not refer to specific people.)

The first-edition foreword listed five articles that were broad treatments of topics: Computer Science, Data Processing, Information Science, Information Processing, and Symbol Manipulation; later editions did not do so. It is not clear now why it specified those articles, as they were not especially long. "Computer Science" was four pages in the 1st edition, though 14 in the 4th. The other articles were about "what computers *do*," as the ones on both data and information processing said, and addressed the multiple ways in which computers handled data, information, or symbols to perform their tasks. The data processing article, which was written by Ralston, also argued that the early distinction between computers for scientific and business calculations was no longer appropriate and may never have been.

While computer science in the narrow sense is an academic discipline, and university departments had taught it for over a decade in 1976, computing in a broader sense had become part of businesses and industry. Some colleges, Dartmouth in particular, had made computer use a part of undergraduate education. People were thus acquainted with computers and computing, if not directly then through numerous reports. From its inception, the ECS thus was intended for multiple audiences, both technical and not—computing had never been solely academic.

Among those audiences were computing professionals, some of whom wrote ECS articles. Anecdotal reports were that they looked at ECS articles in their own fields to assess its accuracy, and assuming favorable judgments about them, looked outside their fields for information about those areas. Ostensibly, college students used the book as a useful reference source and starting point for further reading, and readers outside the computing fields used the book for browsing and education. The editors thought that while there were some quite long technical articles, most were quite broadly accessible.

University libraries were major purchasers of the ECS, and its current edition was commonly in their reference rooms. Although editions were up to date when published, they aged rapidly, and at least in one author's library, the ECS moved to the general collection after a half-decade or so, not long before the next edition appeared. Ralston wrote in 2004 in "Four Editions" that he thought that the ECS also belonged in all high-school libraries, but that only a few acquired it. The editors of the editions after the first agreed and thought also that the book was appropriate for both high-school and college graduates.

In view of broad scope of the term "computer science," it would be very difficult for all encyclopedia articles to be equally accessible to the layperson. Theoretical topics generally require mathematical notation, and though much of it would be intelligible to a high-school graduate, some of it, such as calculus notation, might not be. An account of computer memory would typically involve timing diagrams that would require a reader to be familiar with graphical notation. Descriptions of

---

[25] ECS, 4th edition (Ralston et al. 2000), p. xv.

computer circuitry use symbols for circuit elements, probably unfamiliar to many readers.

Several reviews discuss articles in particular areas, but do not address audience level in general. A review of the ECS and of a multivolume *Encyclopedia of Computer Science and Technology*, edited by Belzer, Holzman, and Kent, in *Computers and Society*[26] praises the ECS for its article classification and indexes, which help the magazine's readers to find topics likely to be of interest. It comments accurately that neither of these works is a dictionary of terms or handbook of computer science, but that the ECS bibliographies and cross-referencing are useful, and that, unlike the multivolume work, the ECS is affordable; but the review does not further address the intended audience. Another review that focuses on the historical articles finds them useful although often too short; it comments that the biographies and articles on early computers provide information not available in any other single place.[27]

A review in the well-known trade magazine *Datamation* looks at the ECS from the standpoint of Ralston's description of it. The reviewer, a computing professional, says that it has considerable breadth as well as depth,[28] and a "rather nice balance struck between the theoretically esoteric and the soiled-hand pragmatic," and adds that its application articles provide an excellent start for a literature search.

A *Datamation* review of the 1983s edition is more critical, saying that the editors did not specify the audience and that the authors wrote for one another, with no consistent level of difficulty, although it does not offer support for that assertion.[29] The reviewer concludes that the book is not appropriate either for the head of a large company that used computers, or for the young and uneducated, and so it has no appropriate audience. (In his "Four editions" article, Ralston remarks that, as his goal was that most of the ECS be accessible to a high-school student, the criticism hurt—particularly as the review attributed the failure to poor editing.)

The advice that ECS editors gave authors included that articles should start with brief definitions or explanations of the topic and that the first part of a long article should be generally accessible even if it eventually became more technical, and the best articles did that well. In the fourth edition, for example, the first page of the eight-page article on compilers (programs that translate a programming language into instructions for a computer to execute) gave a nontechnical introduction describing the steps that a compiler had to undertake, before presenting more detailed sections on each step, followed by a general conclusion. An article on machine translation of human languages has a historical introduction that is similarly accessible, although at one point it uses several technical terms that the editors did not catch. An article on graph theory, a mathematical topic, introduces numerous technical terms but is largely accessible to a high-school math student.

---

[26] Landis 1976.

[27] Tropp 1980.

[28] Granholm 1976.

[29] The review offers the example of the article on complexity that says that the problem has been solved, though the article on (computational) complexity says nothing of the sort, and there is no other evident article on the topic.

2.2 ECS Audience

Like many reference works, the ECS prefaces asked readers to say how future editions could be improved, which articles needed improvement, and what additional topics should be covered; it also asked for corrections. The editors very rarely heard from readers; a few sent minor corrections of names or dates after publication of the 4th edition.

Chapter 3
Stance and Style

Abstract This chapter discusses issues of stance and style in writing an encyclopedia generally and in particular for the *Encyclopedia of Computer Science*. Topics include degree of similarity to other existing reference works, whether scope extends to biography and bibliography, issues of comprehensiveness and selectivity, and interconnectedness of parts of the encyclopedia.

3.1 Encyclopedia Scholars on Stance and Style

Once the decision about audience has been made, the editor still has many other decisions to make about stance and style that may have a profound shaping force on the encyclopedia. One decision to be made is how like or unlike the encyclopedia is to be to the other written reference works: dictionaries, handbooks, biographical collections, or extensive bibliographies.[1] For example, a handbook is generally intended for advanced readers, and, to find the relevant information, the author relies on the reader to consult the table of contents or the index rather than rely upon an alphabetic arrangement of articles.[2] The handbook typically arranges its articles to correspond "to the unified order of ideas."[3] Should the encyclopedia include extensive bibliographies or bibliographic essays; if so, where should they be placed? Should the encyclopedia include biographical articles; if so, of living people only? dead people only? the most famous people only? Should there be a percentage of the book devoted to biographies? Should biographical information be given in other articles?[4] Dictionaries are generally about understanding words while encyclopedias are primarily about understanding events, technologies, and concepts.[5] But will the

---

[1] See Durbin 1996.
[2] Sills 1969, p. 1171.
[3] This wording is taken from France 1998.
[4] See Kallman 1994, p. 8, on the inclusion of biographies of living persons. Sills 1962 and Sills 1969 discuss how an encyclopedia of the social sciences selectively included biographies of thought influencers.
[5] Menagarishvili 2012; Hancher 2019.

encyclopedia editor decide to include entries about particular words or phrases, or about the language of the discipline? The prescriptive versus descriptive issue faced by the dictionary editor is also faced by the encyclopedia editor:

> Traditionally, there have been distinguished two approaches to dictionary making: the descriptive approach that focuses on how the language is used and the prescriptive approach that emphasizes how the language should be used.... At present, the descriptive approach is the guiding principle for the majority of dictionary makers.... according to current literature, the general public stays conservative and expects the dictionary to be prescriptive.[6]

Britannica, *World Book*, and *Funk & Wagnalls* are all examples of general encyclopedias, intended to cover all topics that would be of interest to a literate public. These contrast with area encyclopedias, which cover topics about a particular field of knowledge—often affiliated with a particular academic discipline such as sociology or computer science. Even if one chooses to create an area encyclopedia, there are open issues about the boundary. For example, does an area encyclopedia of computer science include topics concerning how other academic disciplines such as sociology or business might treat computer science, or the applications of computing in other disciplines?[7]

Moreover, how extensive should the encyclopedia be? Should it be comprehensive or selective? Should it appear as one or more than one volume? Should the publisher wait to publish all volumes at the same time?[8] In addition to the question about how interdisciplinary it should be, how broad should its coverage be geographically and chronologically?[9]

Over time, there have been various views of what the encyclopedia should be. In eighteenth-century France, the encyclopedia was intended to be "more a work of art than a work of reference."[10] This sentiment has appeared again in more recent times:

> But the greatest discovery for me was the realization how much lexicography and creative art have in common. True, the one results from observation, the other from imagination. One deals with facts, the other with inventions. One provides knowledge, the other beauty. And yet, lexicographical architecture surely is as much an exercise in creativity as is composition, painting, or play writing. The process of translating a vision inside the mind into an artifact outside that mind, available to other minds, very closely parallels the work of the composer, the painter, the playwright, forever balancing, shaping, leaning back to view detail against the original vision, hoping that in the end all parts will blend into a harmonious whole."[11]

---

[6] Menagarishvili 2012, pp. 5–6. Also see Kallman 1994, p. 8, on being objective versus evaluative.

[7] This question should be broadened to include not only topics from other academic disciplines, but also the approaches adopted by these other disciplines. For example, see Aspray 2024 on many different approaches such as business history, economic history, geographic history, technical history, and policy history. Also see Kallman 1994, p. 7, on the multiplicity of possible approaches. Sills 1962 discusses how these issues about topics across disciplines were handled by an encyclopedia of the social sciences. Kallman 1994 discusses the multiplicity of approaches drawn from history, philology, and ethnology for an encyclopedia of folklore.

[8] France 1998. The 1910 issue of *Britannica* was the first multivolume encyclopedia to have all volumes published simultaneously.

[9] See Rauch 2005; Sills 1962, p. 31.

[10] Van Doren 1962, p. 23.

[11] Kallman 1994, p. 19.

3.1 Encyclopedia Scholars on Stance and Style

According to philosopher Tilottama Rajan, the notebooks of the British Romantic poet Samuel Taylor Coleridge (1772–1834) were more concerned with reflections on the "interconnectedness and incompleteness of knowledge" than with providing "compilation of knowledge."[12] The ethnologist Michaela Fenske has shown how one German encyclopedia of folklore in the 1940s served as a political document, attempting to establish German territorial rights.[13] In 1974 *Britannica* sought to establish a unity of knowledge where none might have existed previously, through a first volume, entitled the *Propaedia*, which explained how the material covered in the rest of the volumes was connected.[14] Barzun ups the pressure on the encyclopedia editor: "the task of preparing a new encyclopedia suddenly appears as the embodiment of the greatest intellectual problem of the age: to keep the bulk of human knowledge common property by keeping it communicable."[15]

In addition to discussions about what an encyclopedia should be, encyclopedia historians have considered various means of achieving these goals: pleasurable writing;[16] illustrations;[17] broad overview articles and organizational aids to readers,[18] variations in depth of coverage for general concepts and specific embodiments thereof,[19] theory articles that discuss the principles under which the encyclopedia was organized,[20] discussions of the importance of institutions,[21] making most articles accessible to the reader,[22] the value of including advanced topics for the sake of making them known even if they will be beyond the full understanding of most

---

[12] Rajan 2007, p 336.

[13] Fenske 2010.

[14] See the discussion in Yeo 1991. Van Doren 1962, p. 23, discusses the encyclopedia providing a "synthesis", an "underlying theory". He goes on to write: "Because the world is radically new, the ideal encyclopedia should be radical, too. It should stop being safe—in politics, in philosophy, in science. It should create a synthesis where none is thought to be possible. It should carve a new order out of the chaos that has swept away the old. It should think of itself as an important—perhaps even the most important tool for the reconstruction of a world where has meaning." (p. 26) See Rajan 2007 on the consolidation, professionalization, specialization, and disaggregation going on in Britannica. And see Durbin 1996 on several examples through history where encyclopedists have attempted to achieve the orderly integration of knowledge.

[15] Barzun 1962, p. 7.

[16] Barzun 1962; France 1998.

[17] Kallman 1994.

[18] Sullivan 1990.

[19] See, for example, the discussion in Yeo 1991 of the 3rd edition of *Britannica*.

[20] Couch 1962, p. 21; also see Yeo 1991 reflecting on how scientific disciplines embrace agreed upon divisions of knowledge.

[21] Menagarishvili 2012.

[22] Durbin 1996.

readers,[23] the importance of the inclusion of unfamiliar topics,[24] and the value found in formatting practices such as use of columns, bold headings, and endnotes.[25]

The English word "encyclopedia" comes from the Greek phrase *enkyklios paideia*, which translates as "complete instruction."[26] Several encyclopedia scholars have pointed to the importance for encyclopedias that they are authoritative. If, as one encyclopedia scholar stated, "Clearly, encyclopedias function as external memories. They are a resource for epistemic information that makes it unnecessary to remember details since those can be looked up,"[27] then their authority is important to assure the correctness of these memories. For traditional encyclopedias, authority is achieved through the quality reputation of the publisher, the acknowledged expertise of the entry authors and the editors, and the careful editorial process.[28] Another encyclopedia scholar pointed out that, over time, the locus of authority shifted from the editors or the scholar who wrote the philosophical unity of knowledge preface to the collective group of experts who wrote the articles.[29]

3.2 ECS Stance and Style

The ECS was designed as a single-volume area encyclopedia, with entries alphabetically organized. It had no predecessors in its field, although in scope and organization it resembled other area encyclopedias. It may have been a product of negotiations among scholars as Fenske says,[30] though we do not know what transpired among its editorial board or authors. It was a product of its time by virtue of existing, i.e., due to the growing interest in computing. Contrary to Charles van Doren's assertion that "American encyclopedias do not have a mission" and are "essentially conservative,"[31] the ECS did bring "order out of chaos"[32] through its structure, though "chaos" is an overly strong term for a discipline that was still in the process of formation.

The 1st edition embodied that structure in a four-level taxonomy of all articles into ten categories, with articles split roughly evenly between the third and fourth levels.

---

[23] Van Doren 1962, pp. 23–24.

[24] In a discussion of dictionaries that is clearly transferrable to encyclopedias, Menagarishvili 2012, p. 18, writes: "Dictionaries render the new information mobile, keep it stable, and are combinable, therefore, they can be the means that help 'bring home' the unfamiliar." In the case of an encyclopedia of computer science, think for example of the Antikythera mechanism or of the counting measures of a remote South American tribe.

[25] Fenske 2010.

[26] Wexelbaum 2012, p. 7.

[27] Haider and Sundin 2014, p. 8.

[28] Haider and Sundin 2014; also see Barzun 1962 on the need of authors to be not only area experts but also good expositors of their subject.

[29] Yeo 1991.

[30] Fenske 2010, p. 64.

[31] Van Doren 1962, p. 26.

[32] Van Doren 1962.

3.2 ECS Stance and Style

Table. 3.1 *Encyclopedia of computer science* taxonomy

First edition	Later editions
Hardware	Hardware
Computer systems	Computer systems
Software	Information and data
Basic terminology	Software
Theory	Theory of computation
Mathematics for computer science	Mathematics of computer science
Applications	Applications
Management, societal, economic, and legal aspects	Methodologies
Professional and educational aspects	Computing Milieux [including history]
History	

Subsequent editions had nine categories; in the fourth edition, the software category was split into three second levels: Programming and programming languages, software engineering, and systems software. Table 3.1 lists the two taxonomies. The 4th edition taxonomy comprised some 850 entries, the majority at level 3, which meant that some of its 623 articles appear more than once; for example, the compiler article falls under both programming languages and systems software.

This taxonomy also became the basis for the computer science taxonomy that the now-defunct American Federation of Information Processing Societies adopted in 1980; and it is like the taxonomy that the Association for Computing Machinery uses today. According to Ralston,[33] he developed the taxonomy, but he does not indicate how much he may have consulted with the ECS editorial board.

The ACM curricular guidelines provide a different organization of the computer science discipline. They first appeared in 1968 and have been revised roughly every decade. Its categories are a subset of the ECS taxonomy, being at the course-subject level and hence coarser; and they are also largely restricted to the technical aspects of computing. These guidelines went through several iterations, and the 1991 version was strongly influenced by a 1988 joint ACM-IEEE report, "Computing as a Discipline."[34] The report characterizes the discipline as including three focuses (called "paradigms" or "processes"): theory, abstraction (modeling), and design. The lead author, Peter Denning, also wrote the extensive "Computer science" article in the 4th edition of the ECS, which follows the report quite closely.

The finding aids that the first edition offered for its quite broad variety of articles included extensive indexes. The early editions each contained a single index, with

---

[33] Anthony Ralston, oral history interview, William Aspray and Bernard de Neumann, interviewers, ACM Oral History Interviews, January 10, 2006 (https://doi.org/10.1145/1141880.1147774). At one point, Ralston says that the AFIPS taxonomy, on which he worked, was the source of the ECS taxonomy, although in his 2004 Annals article, he says the reverse, which is the more plausible, as the ECS appeared in 1976 and the AFIPS taxonomy in 1980.

[34] See Denning, et al. 1989.

about 4500 entries in the first edition. The third and fourth editions included separate name and general indexes; in the fourth edition, the name index included about 2900 entries and the general index about 7500. The latter served also as a dictionary of computing, with entries for commonly used terms.

The ECS ordered articles alphabetically by the words most likely to be sought, with cross-references for titles that might have more than one such search term. Article headings had cross-referenced lists of related articles, and their texts had "see" or "q.v" for terms that were the titles of their own articles. The combination of these cross-references and the extensive indexes made it generally easy to find topics when they were not evident in the alphabetical ordering.

So far as we know, Ralston did not consult encyclopedias in other areas when planning the ECS, although its alphabetical organization was quite standard. Unlike some encyclopedias that are called *dictionaries*, e.g., the *Harvard Dictionary of Music*,[35] it did not have entries that were merely definitions. Contrary to Couch,[36] who argued that an encyclopedia should have articles on the theory of its organization, the ECS did not have such articles, but drew on commonly held views of members of the discipline as they were expressed in technical publications.

A related category of reference work is the handbook, addressed to professionals rather than general readers, and organized by topic rather than alphabetically. For one comparison, the *Computer Science Handbook*[37] has 13 chapters in its algorithms section. The ECS taxonomy has 15 entries under "algorithm", nine of which are not under "A". Half of them match or closely correspond to the *Handbook* chapters, however, and several of the others have clear connections. Most contain cross-references in their headings. For example, "Algorithms, Analysis of" and "NP-complete Problem" each refers to the other, so that the effect is to comprehend the handbook organization quite effectively.

There were also appendices. The first edition had a seven-page appendix of abbreviations of organization names and technical terms; together with several mathematical tables, including a nicely triangular table of powers of 2 and their reciprocals. The second edition added lists of computer science journals and of academic departments, major programming languages, and perhaps most important a glossary of terms in English, French, German, Russian, and Spanish. The third and fourth editions added a timeline of computing with occasional entries intended as humorous, such as:

> 1540 Robert Recorde invents the equal sign, "=," and, as a matter of recorde, turns over in his grave when it is ambiguously used as the replacement operator in *Fortran* and *C++*.

In the fourth edition, the list of abbreviations grew to 29 pages, while the mathematical tables were limited to notation and Greek-prefixed units such as nanosecond and gigabyte. The appendix of journals was 13 pages long, and the departments appendix was five pages and listed department Web sites. There was a new appendix

---

[35] Randell 2003.
[36] Couch 1962, p. 21.
[37] Tucker 2004.

of presidents of major organizations, and another that listed articles of earlier editions that had been deleted.

Article bibliographies were short, typically from several to about ten entries, primarily of current books except for some historical articles. These lists served as recommendations for further reading rather than as extensive documentation of articles; in this respect, the ECS was distinguished from a handbook addressed to professionals.

The editors were members of computer science departments, with expertise in algorithms and computing mathematics (Ralston), programming and computer center administration (Reilly), and in programming languages, computer architecture, and parallel computing (Hemmendinger); all three were also interested in computing history. Together, they were capable of editing the broad range of ECS articles, though the authority of the book stemmed from the authority vested in its authors.

A minor feature that distinguished the ECS from some other encyclopedias, such as the *Encyclopaedia Britannica*, is that articles gave authors' full names, with a list of them and their affiliations at the front of the book. Contrary to the practice of some encyclopedias that sign articles with initials, the author list was alphabetized by last name rather than by first initial, which would be far less useful for looking up an author. Although it was probably of interest primarily to scholars in the field, the editors considered it important support for the authority of the ECS.

The ECS was interdisciplinary in its including topics beyond strict computer science, and computer science is itself somewhat interdisciplinary according to the "Computing as a Discipline" report;[38] the ECS covered its three aspects: theory, abstraction, and design. Its interdisciplinary character extended to uses of computing in many fields and to computing history; it was less broad in its geographical coverage, being largely about the USA and Western Europe.

In view of the diversity of what is called "computer science", and in view of the ongoing academic discussions of what constitutes its core, the goal of the ECS was not to establish a unity of knowledge, which may have been the purpose of some encyclopedias. Nevertheless, the quote from Jacques Barzun in an earlier section is appropriate: a major purpose of the ECS from its start 50 years ago was to help to make and keep the bulk of knowledge of computing fields common property by keeping it communicable.

As we mentioned in an earlier section, from the start the ECS had covered more than technical aspects of computing; it devoted articles to societal functions as well, as reflected in the titles of several of its major sections. Its first edition included 13 historical articles, all concerning early computers, and 16 biographies. The fourth edition had 51 historical articles, many but no longer all concerning early machines, including ten on programming languages. There are 38 biographies, and the editors had decided not to include any new ones on living people, unlike earlier editions.

The editors sought to keep articles neutral with respect to controversies. A few articles by major computer scientists were somewhat idiosyncratic and opinionated (e.g., by Jean Sammet and Eric Weiss, two long-time writers of computing history),

---

[38] Denning 1989.

but most of the articles are not primarily evaluative, except in so far as the material they include reflects an evaluation. Later editions preserved those few articles by opinionated authors, although by the time of the fourth edition, the authors or editors did update them, while trying to preserve their idiosyncratic tone.

Successive editions paid increasing attention to societal aspects of computing, although that was there from the start, along with technical articles. Among these were the "Society, Computers in" article, "Women in Computing", "Computer Ethics", and on "Legal Aspects of Computing." The articles commented on disagreements while largely remaining neutral. One on automation, for example, mentioned extreme views of it as either entirely beneficial or as wholly deleterious, while commenting that they both treated automation as autonomous, even though it was a social process that could be evaluated in multiple ways.

Appropriately for a reference work, the ECS articles addressed reasonably well-established topics rather than ones regarded at the time as marginal or not well established. The first two editions included no article on bulletin boards or computer conferencing, while the last two editions did—including an article by Murray Turoff, one of its main proponents. The fourth edition had no article on digital or online encyclopedias, although prior to Wikipedia, they were not a very distinct category. Cellular telephony was treated in the article on communication and computing, but smart phones were not yet an established type, although by the early 1990s, there were phones that retrospectively might be called "smart." By not having articles on the very latest developments, the ECS no doubt missed some that became important, but it also avoided treating topics that proved evanescent, such as "B2B" (business-to-business) computing, a buzzword in the late 1990s, which the editors considered covering, although it later became just another aspect of computer networking. ECS has no article on any of the sorts of informal or "underground" uses of computing, such as Joy Rankin discusses in her historical scholarship,[39] even though that would have been an appropriate topic.

---

[39] Rankin 2018.

Chapter 4
Content

Abstract This chapter discusses issues of content in writing an encyclopedia generally and in particular for the *Encyclopedia of Computer Science*. Topics include whether to include only the current state of knowledge or also an examination of the history of the field, standards for factual reporting, depth of content provided, and whether to provide a systematic overview of the field or readily accessible independent entries on topics.

4.1 Encyclopedia Scholars on Content

Many encyclopedia scholars have written about the types of content essential in an encyclopedia. We summarize their thoughts by focusing on two apparent conflicts in their claims about encyclopedias. The first is that these scholars argue that encyclopedias are both scientific documents and historical documents. But many of today's scholars would argue that while scientific documents have historical contexts, their contents are *ahistorical*. To resolve this possible conflict requires unpacking what these encyclopedia scholars mean by these two terms.

Let us first consider the encyclopedia as a scientific text. These scholars do not mean that all encyclopedias are full of scientific facts and theories—though an encyclopedia of physics might be. They also do not mean that an encyclopedia is created according to methods of the natural sciences, such as empirical or hypothetico-deductive methods that historians and philosophers of science have discussed as typical. Nor do they mean that the information included in an encyclopedia would stand up to verifiability or falsifiability tests; these encyclopedia scholars are not referring to either Francis Bacon or Karl Popper when they apply the descriptor "scientific".

When these scholars discuss the encyclopedia as a "scientific" text, they instead refer to the consistent application of standards about which facts concerning the world should be included (but, secondarily, also alluding to how powerful natural science has been in revealing facts about the world).[1] As the historian Jacques Barzun explains:

> an encyclopedia is first and foremost a work of reference. Its chief use is bound to be as a set of answers to questions about matters of historical or scientific fact— names, places, dates, relationships, titles of books, terms of art, definitions, ideas and principles, formulas, distinctions between cognate systems, compendious records of lives, deeds, and their consequences, descriptions of methods of inquiry and delimitations of fields of knowledge—all this and more, presented in the briefest form compatible with clarity.[2]

He adds that this material needs to be put into context: "And since no subject is ever wholly separable from its neighbors, or intelligible without them, each must be adroitly and exactly placed in the natural setting of its nearest kin."[3] The editor W. T. Couch makes a similar point, drawing on the thoughts of other major figures from American intellectual history for confirmation:

> I am inclined to agree with Henry Adams that "nothing in education is so astonishing as the amount of ignorance it collects in the form of inert facts." I am inclined to agree with Morris Cohen—and many others—that "facts are meaningless except as parts of a system."[4]

What do these scholars mean when they refer to the encyclopedia as a historical document? They do not mean that the goal of the encyclopedia is to make a systematic study of the past, leading to a narrative or interpretation of past events. These encyclopedias would not be recognized as historical texts by modern philosophers of history such as Paul Ricoeur or Hayden White. Instead, they mean that topics are covered in the encyclopedia in a systematic way that admits the coverage of information discovered at many different times—even if some of it has subsequently been demonstrated to be inaccurate or incomplete (e.g., the heliocentric Copernican theories); and to describe past events, as warranted, to help the reader to understand a particular event or concept that appears as an entry in the encyclopedia (e.g., astronomical theories of the solar system).

As Couch observes about encyclopedias: "Unlike other works, their job is to report facts and theories of all kinds. If they do their job, they are historical works that are as inclusive as possible with space apportioned to subjects in accord with their importance."[5] Jacques Barzun argues that inclusion should be for those ideas that stand the test of time, or in his words, "...ideas and issues are alike to be refined historically. The great ideas are those that have engaged the protracted attention of

---

[1] As Yeo 1991, p. 26, explains: "Since the eighteenth century there has been a strong correlation between the multiplication of encyclopedias and the growth of scientific knowledge. Most of the encyclopedias published from this time gave an important place to science and technology-they were often called dictionaries of arts and sciences; subjects such as biography, history, geography, and literature were usually later additions."

[2] Barzun 1962, p. 8. Also see Yeo 1991 on the long history, since the early nineteenth century, of extensive coverage of scientific disciplines in encyclopedias.

[3] Barzun 1962, p. 8.

[4] Couch 1962, p. 19.

[5] Couch 1962, p. 20.

mankind."[6] Richard Yeo notes that this notion of the encyclopedia has rich origins in the history of Western thought:

> This recourse to a historical framework was not peculiar to the *Britannica*. In fact, the idea of a chronological or historical presentation of knowledge has strong Baconian affiliations and was contrasted by seventeenth-century writers with the logically deductive mode of scholasticism. Chambers saw the historical mode of exposition as the most suitable for a dictionary or encyclopedia: "The Dictionary ... supposes the advances and discoveries made, and processed to explain or relate them. The Lexicographer, like an historian, comes after the affair; and gives a description of what passed."[7]

These unorthodox definitions of scientific text and historical text are not in contradiction—as one can readily see. One might say what they mean is that encyclopedias are composed in a systematic way, including material about the past.

The various scholars of the encyclopedia point to a second apparent conflict in the creation of an encyclopedia: between being selective and avoiding biases. On the one hand, there is potentially so much material to cover, and there must be some principles that guide the inclusion selection process. As Lawrence Sullivan argues:

> Culling and organizing whatever is known of such an enormous variety of subjects, over the many years required to prepare encyclopedic works, can hardly be done without some overarching goal, some hope of making a point, or at least without reflecting on the relationship of knowledge to truth and the impact of such truth on individual and social life and the direction of history.[8]

Using an encyclopedia of religion as an example, Sullivan goes on to explain that it may be necessary to include in the encyclopedia material that would normally appear to be too academic for an encyclopedia, as both a way to explain the guiding principle for topical inclusion and a way to illustrate the ways of thinking of academics:

> The third conceptual block that underlies the *Encyclopedia of Religion* is given to the study of religion itself. Here one finds lengthy essays on theories of religion and on the conceptual tools developed to study it. [Mircea] Eliade felt that a close examination of methods in the study of religion was essential, not simply so that scholars could narcissistically turn their attention to scholarship within their own profession, but because theories of religion are one way in which our own historical epoch has reflected on religious experience.[9]

On the other hand, the encyclopedia should "by its very nature avoid becoming a manifesto of any parochial intellectual position [but instead]...strive toward catholicity."[10] Various means might be used to achieve this catholicity, such as a conscious effort by the editor to seek topics at the boundary of the field to round out the article list, or broaden the article contributor list to include many non-Americans,[11] as well as dissenters from orthodoxy.

---

[6] Barzun 1962, p. 9.
[7] Yeo 1991, p. 33. Footnote number in original removed.
[8] Sullivan 1990, p. 317.
[9] Sullivan 1990, p. 338.
[10] Sills 1962, p. 31.
[11] Sills 1969.

Encyclopedias are serious, labor-intensive enterprises—these scholars observe—serious in the sense of giving a systematic understanding of their entire subject area, not just popularizing knowledge. As Yeo argues in *Isis*, "In contrast to their successors, encyclopedias of the early nineteenth century carried articles that were effectively pieces of original research at the leading edge of various fields."[12] The eighteenth-century English encyclopedist Ephraim Chambers worried that if encyclopedias fell down on their job in the face of ever-growing amounts of information, "the progress of science would be handicapped because those who should make discoveries would have to spend their 'whole life learning what is already found out' ... and that certain 'inventions and improvements' might 'sink into oblivion.'"[13] By the late nineteenth century, there were other venues for the publication of cutting-edge research, notably journals; but this does not mean the objective of the encyclopedia devolved to mere popularization.[14] They were still intended to be a place where a reader could find authoritative knowledge of the topics in question.

4.2 ECS Content

How did the ECS balance the competing demands of scientific rigor and historical accuracy on the one hand, and those of selectivity—having a point of view—and freedom from bias on the other hand? We know little about how Ralston and his editorial board made their decisions for the first edition. The article classification scheme includes the expected computer science topics in hardware and software, computer theory, and mathematics. Its list of computing applications in other disciplines fills half a column, while the fourth edition list is nearly two columns. "History" occupies less than a column, but nearly two columns in the fourth edition. By contrast, the sections on computing mathematics are about the same length in both editions, though a few entries differ. This section includes topics that, though important for numerical computation, are quite general, such as approximation theory and least-squares approximation. The treatment may reflect Ralston's background in mathematics.

There were naturally some changes in emphasis and new topics that the 1976 edition could not yet cover. Analog computing was reduced from 22 pages in the first edition to six in the fourth. Personal computing was not a topic in the first edition; more surprisingly, neither was robotics, which had only a brief paragraph in the article on artificial intelligence. That edition included a text-editing article, but

---

[12] Yeo 1991, p. 26.

[13] Yeo 1991, p. 28.

[14] However, as Kallman 1994 (p. 8) explains in his discussion of the Canadian music encyclopedia, it can be challenging to provide all the information needed by the various types of readers of the encyclopedia: "We wanted our readers to acquire recordings and printed music, to proceed to further reading and research, and to plan their studies, competition entries, or festival attendances. Hence the many lists or statistics of archival and library holdings, and of periodicals, festivals, awards, instrument collections, community orchestras, courses and degrees given at various universities, and so forth."

none on word processing or desktop publishing, and neither topic was listed in the index. By the fourth edition, however, there were articles on these topics, as well as ones on markup languages and the TeX text-formatting system.

The early editions had more brief articles that defined a term in its computing context than did the later editions, which generally subsumed them under broader topics. Some such brief articles described a specialized sense of a common word, such as "backtracking", "fix", "feasibility study", and "noise". Others introduced computing terminology that seemed more significant at the time than it did later, e.g., "dangling else" (an ambiguity in some programming language definitions), "compiler, incremental" and "compiler, syntax-directed" that later were incorporated into a general article on compilers that might have been there from the start. Yet others just did not seem important later, such as "computer, using a", "database administrator". An appendix in the fourth edition listed all articles deleted from previous editions, noting which had been subsumed under current articles (it would have been useful also to have lists of when articles were introduced). Table 4.1 has some examples of articles deleted from early editions.

One way to examine how *au courant* the ECS was is to look at professional publications. The *Communications of the ACM* is the flagship magazine of the Association

Table 4.1 Some examples of deleted articles

Article	Last in edition	Replacement, if any
Computer, using a	1	
Computing economics: acquisition and operation	1	
Copyrights and patents, computer aspects of	1	*See* Legal protection of software
Operation code	1	*See* Instruction set
Planning systems, characteristics of	1	
Addressless instructions	2	
ARPA network	2	*See* Networks, computer
Controlled variable	2	
Credit systems applications	2	
Feasibility study	2	
Fix	2	
Command and job control language	3	
Computer-managed instruction	3	
Computing center	3	
One-level memory	3	
Operations research	3	
Turnaround time	3	
Turnkey	3	

of Computing Machinery, and *Computer*, that of the IEEE Computer Society—the two major computing societies in the United States. In the early 1970s, the former was primarily a technical publication, but by the 1990s it was broader and addressed both academic and industry computer practitioners with articles on currently important topics. Tables 4.2 and 4.3 list the topics that the magazine covers illustrated during 1995, when work began on the fourth edition.

The ECS addressed many of these topics. The third edition was the first to have an article on women in computing, and the fourth edition expanded it. Asynchronous transfer mode (ATM) has a fourth-edition article, as in the early 1990s it appeared to be important, although less so by the end of the decade. The fourth edition added six-page articles on digital libraries and on cognitive science. The third edition had added an article on object-oriented programming, which had become important by the early 1980s; the fourth expanded it moderately and added another on object-oriented analysis and design. It also added one on computer ethics, which it supplemented an earlier one on computer crime, and one on multimedia that included discussion of hypermedia (extending hypertext to multiple media). Many of these topics were addressed in other articles as well. Topics in Table 4.2 that did not have their own articles, such as those concerning AI, were addressed, for example, in articles on artificial intelligence, neural networks, multi-agent systems, machine learning, and

Table 4.2 1995 *Communications of the ACM* cover topics

Women in computing
Asynchronous transfer mode (ATM)
Uncertainty in AI; Bayesian methods
Digital libraries
Requirements gathering
Cognition and software development
End-user training and learning
Designing hypermedia applications
Representations of work
Object-oriented experiences and future trends
New horizons in commercial and industrial AI
Ethics and computer use

Table 4.3 1995 *IEEE Computer* magazine cover topics

Road to software maturity
The time crunch: rapid prototyping
Visual programming
Organizing client/server computing
Multimedia
Scheduling and real-time systems
Virtual environments
Where is software heading?
Finding the right image: content-based image retrieval
Object-oriented technology
Parallel and distributed processing tools
Evaluating software systems

fuzzy logic. Some of the topics in the table concern how to organize computer-related work and were addressed at least indirectly in articles on software design and engineering, though not explicitly.

Several of the Table 4.3 topics are also addressed in articles devoted at least in part to them: multimedia, real-time systems, client/server computing, rapid prototyping, object-oriented technology, and parallel and distributed computing. Others concern professional practices in software development, to which the ECS gave less attention, though it covered the fundamentals of software design.

A topic that might have received more attention is content-based image retrieval, which the articles on information retrieval and digital libraries could have addressed but did not; in the late 1990s, it was still a new topic. An area that could have been addressed better is the human and societal impact of software projects, especially large ones. The article on computers in society did discuss reliability and risk, including some software failures, such as the well-documented Therac-25 X-ray machine that killed several patients, and an article on the Computer Professionals for Social Responsibility organization mentioned its opposition to the Strategic Defense Initiative. These or similar topics were not discussed in articles on software safety or others on software, reflecting a split between the more technical articles and those on human issues.

To judge from these limited selections, the ECS had a reasonable approach: it was not at the forefront in promoting new technology, but it added articles on topics that were becoming important in the field. Similarly, it was attentive to societal issues such as the status of women in computing fields, but did not promote particular causes.

An example of a topic that the ECS might have covered but did not is wireless networking. The IEEE 802.11 standard that defined the so-called wi-fi protocol was established in 1997, when fourth-edition articles had been commissioned, although the idea had been discussed since the late 1980s, and an Australian project had demonstrated it in the early 1990s.[15] A comprehensive article on communications and computers did mention wireless in connection with cellular telephony and suggested that it would lead to wireless networking. The editors rejected some new articles proposed by reviewers as being too technical or too narrow; a currently popular topic that they considered but rejected was "B2B" (business to business) communication, and it did not prove of lasting importance. The "dot-com boom" was under way as the edition was in process, but neither it nor its collapse at about the time of publication was addressed by the ECS. It did have an article on the "Y2K" problem, which described the problem that arose at the end of 1999 due to representing years with only two digits, and was prudently noncommittal in predicting its effects.

There were also missed opportunities to present the historical context of important ideas. Some of the features of contemporary computing systems were introduced quite early in digital computer history. These include instruction-level parallelism (ILP), in which a computer CPU can execute more than one instruction at once, either due to a pipeline of instructions under way or to its having multiple arithmetic

---

[15] O'Sullivan 2018.

units; and cache memory, which puts frequently used storage in the fastest memory elements. Articles on early computers, such as the 1961 IBM Stretch and the 1964 CDC 6600, mentioned their use of ILP, but the article on ILP has nothing on this history. Cache memory is very important in speeding instruction execution today, but while it was introduced in 1965, that history is not in the fourth-edition article on the topic, although it was briefly mentioned in the third edition. Other articles, however, do provide that historical context; for example, one on microprogramming, a technique for implementing a CPU instruction set, traces its origin to 1951.

We should consider how the editors' backgrounds may have affected their decisions. None of the three fourth-edition editors had Ph.D.s in computer science, though all were or had been in computer science departments: Ralston's Ph.D. was in mathematics (1956), Reilly's in physics (1969), and Hemmendinger's in philosophy (1973). The last had a M.S. in computer science (1982) and unlike the other two was still teaching the subject. He was probably the best-informed about the current state of the subject, particularly in the more technical areas—computer architecture, programming languages, operating systems, networking—though less so in personal-computing applications. All three were attentive to societal issues and matters of public policy, often relying on reviewers for author recommendations.

The ECS largely adopted prevailing views of computing outside the United States. Its article on the computer industry had a long section on the United States and shorter ones on Britain, Western Europe, and Japan. The computer-education article also had a long section on the United States, which included discussion of ACM and IEEE curricular guidelines, with short sections on Europe and Asia. There was no mention of the Indian information technology industry, although much of its growth occurred after publication of the ECS. The article and the appendix on computer societies was somewhat more broadly international, although Australia got no mention. Historical computers in the United States, Britain, France, and Germany had articles or mentions, but not those in Australia, the Soviet Union, or Japan.

In summary, the ECS was quite systematic in its treatment of computer science topics, as well as societal issues, particularly in the later editions. It was also attentive to the historical origins of computing, primarily as they were related to contemporary digital computing, although with some attention to other topics, such as mechanical calculators. Its point of view was largely consistent with how the discipline understood itself, particularly regarding the emphasis on developments in the United States and Western Europe; if there were to be a new edition now, it would probably pay more attention to other parts of the world.

Chapter 5
The Editorial Process

Abstract This chapter discusses the editorial process in writing an encyclopedia generally and in particular for the *Encyclopedia of Computer Science*. Topics include determining guidelines for writing style, identifying appropriate authors, and interacting with authors, including making them adhere to deadlines and writing guidelines.

5.1 Encyclopedia Scholars on the Editorial Process

The editor or editors of an encyclopedia must make numerous decisions about the desired content and style and enforce those decisions uniformly at every stage in the creation or recreation of the text as they interact with the article authors, the editorial board, and the publisher. Otherwise, the encyclopedia is likely to be inconsistent and ineffective.

There are many issues that the editors must decide upon and enforce. Some of the most common examples include: the writing style, e.g., how telegraphic the writing is and how technical the language can be;[1] styles of argumentation to employ;[2] how didactic articles should be;[3] how much to homogenize the styles of the tens or hundreds of different authors;[4] the precision of factual information, such as the

---

[1] Kallman 1994.

[2] Fenske 2010 discusses how challenging this task is in the humanities, where styles of argumentation differ from one academic discipline to the next, and how styles of argumentation in these disciplines can change rapidly over time. These issues bear upon the reader's reception of the authoritativeness and the up-to-datedness of the encyclopedia.

[3] On this issue, Barzun 1962 (pp. 8–9) opines: "But no surer way could be found to render the work at once tedious and suspect than to obtrude the didactic intention beyond that of supplying answers to questions of fact and meaning. Indeed, one could go farther and state as a general proposition that the task is not to get a subject treated and then surround it with enticing foreign matter, like a tomato in aspic but to employ as writers men who understand their subject and also the world in which the subject grows."

[4] Kallman 1994. Rajan 2007 also discusses the issues of dividing the writing across multiple authors.

dates and places discussed in articles;[5] methods for enabling compactness such as "simplifying language, using abbreviations, and eliminating duplications by cross-referencing to other articles with related contents;"[6] deciding on boundaries for individual articles and for inclusion of topics in the encyclopedia;[7] choosing between having some articles on sweeping topics and a larger number of articles on more focused topics;[8] being flexible in determining and enforcing word length of an article so as to include essential information but avoid padding;[9] insisting that authors evaluate fairly and sufficiently the contributions of living persons;[10] providing overview articles or comments within articles that indicate how topics covered in different articles are interrelated;[11] balancing recitation of facts with elaboration of related ideas;[12] avoiding political and other bias in individual articles and across the articles;[13] deciding whether to reprint or revise articles from previous encyclopedias, including in some cases earlier editions of the same encyclopedia;[14] and deciding whether to produce a single- or multiple-volume encyclopedia in the face of a growing body of scholarship in the field covered by the encyclopedia.[15]

Another set of issues for the editing of an encyclopedia concern the choice and makeup of the editorial team, or the editorial process more generally, not specifically

---

[5] Kallman 1994.

[6] Kallman 1994, p. 16. Also see Yeo 1991 on means to avoid duplication across articles.

[7] Kallman 1994, p. 9.

[8] Kallman 1994, p. 10. On broad synthetic articles in an encyclopedia, Barzun 1962 (p. 9) writes: "The world-wide encyclopedia would bury its best assets if it attempted to secure broad synthetic articles on ideas or issues corresponding to the recognized classifications of knowledge. The assignment of such articles makes systematic editing difficult and moreover encourages the writer to abuse the privilege of being doctrinaire. This is natural enough: in writing a panoramic essay he forgets the nature of encyclopedic communication and falls into the composition of chapters that are to bear his mark as well as his signature. No longer a compiler and contributor, he is an author and a symposiast."

[9] Kallman 1994, p. 11.

[10] Kallman 1994, p. 8.

[11] France 1998. In earlier encyclopedias, such as those by Chambers or Diderot, there were extensive tools such as long essays, tables, and trees of knowledge that elaborated on the interconnection of topics covered in various articles (see France 1998).

[12] Barzun 1962 (p. 9) colorfully discusses the interplay of issues and ideas in an encyclopedia article: "Certainly, to provide the two great elements requisite to understanding–Issues and Ideas– no amount of patching and plastering after the fact will avail. Ideas cannot be laid on like icing on top of dry factual articles, nor can issues be pulled out like plums from a pudding into which they were not put while it was being made. For the 'great' articles (or at least the big ones), the writer must possess a philosophic mind to begin with."

[13] To set this issue of bias in relief, France 1998 (p. 73) discusses the ready acknowledgement by the editor of a nineteenth century encyclopedia: "his republican and left-wing sympathies clearly feature in numerous entries. He makes no bones of this type of commitment, remarking in his preface that 'a historical dictionary which is published in the middle of the nineteenth century is bound to share the emancipatory ideas of the age.'"

[14] Sills 1962, p. 32.

[15] Sills 1962, p. 32; Sills 1969, p. 1169.

5.1 Encyclopedia Scholars on the Editorial Process

about issues related to content in the encyclopedia. Even for single-volume encyclopedias, the scale of the enterprise is typically beyond the capability of a single editor to complete in a few years.[16] Larger encyclopedias might require tens or even hundreds of people—with a variety of skills and responsibilities working together for as much as a decade. For example, in his encyclopedia of music in Canada, Kallman described his staffing and their responsibilities:

> [We] assembled a staff, as the need for research, record-keeping, or typing arose [of] twelve salaried and six part-time or occasional workers, all keenly motivated and strongly dedicated to the project. Although each had prescribed responsibilities, everyone regardless of rank was encouraged to note errors, suggest additional entries or deletions, or criticize what one of us had written—nothing mattered but to create the best possible text. Contributors, translators, and other assistants were paid on a piece basis. [There were also some volunteers].[17]

The task of producing an encyclopedia involved "ready source material, competent scholars, and generous scholarship."[18] Recordkeeping and timetable were significant issues,[19] if the process of drafting the content took too long, the earliest articles written for this encyclopedia might need revision to bring them up to date.[20] Another editor of a major encyclopedia, David Sills, summarized the issues faced in doing detailed editorial work:

> We were responsible for extracting articles from intellectually nervous or overcommitted professors; for negotiating with the publisher several times a year on the budget and the production schedule; for acting as gadflies in keeping some of the field editors attentive to the needs of the encyclopedia; for determining rules for stylistic matters and writing a style book with which to enforce them; for making a policy for quotations, citations, and bibliographies and establishing procedures to ensure their accuracy; for devising procedures to verify the many thousand cross references; for writing guides to related articles to place at the head of articles on broad topics; for instructing the printer on how to set complicated mathematical matter in linotype; and for seemingly endless proofreading.[21]

The most suitable places for the creation of an encyclopedia in the twentieth century were "special environments such as those offered by established universities, well-stocked libraries, or major research institutes."[22] There was also the important issue to consider of the background, experiences, and other qualifications of the lead editor. This issue was revealingly discussed regarding the choice of Will-Erich Peuckert to be the lead editor of a well-known folklore encyclopedia in the 1960s. Peuckert had an impressive background as a scholar:

---

[16] The first edition of ECS is an exception.

[17] Kallman 1994, pp. 10-11.

[18] Kallman 1994, p. 4.

[19] As Kallman 1994 (p. 12) described his process: "Administrative staff kept fastidious records of assignments and due dates, dates of submissions received and passed on to editors, and dates of final typing and payment of contributors. Statistics of assignments, completions, editions, and translations, enabled the staff and board to measure progress against previous estimates and to set new target dates."

[20] Kallman 1994, p. 16.

[21] Sills 1969, p. 1171.

[22] Fenske 2010, p. 66.

Before the war, Peuckert was regarded as a promising researcher, full of power and charisma. Indeed, Peuckert was prolific: he published drama, scientific biographies, and monographs, a number of them dealing with the tremendously exciting premodern world or culture of agrarian societies. ... During this time Peuckert developed his characteristic style of writing and reasoning, narrating history in a fresh manner that was readable for a broad audience, arguing from the inside of former worlds, mixing sources and scientific writing into his special form of narration. [However,] Peuckert's mix of fact and fiction in his encyclopedia constituted one entry point for subsequent critique.[23]

Some of the various stakeholders (e.g., editors, academics, funders, and publishers) argued that Peuckert was not the right person for this project.[24] For example, he resisted calls from his publishers and funders, but eventually gave in to create "a complete and detailed list of subject headings" as foundational to the project.[25] Indeed, as another encyclopedia scholar noted, the lead editor had to have not only a broad knowledge of the subject area, but also a "thick skin":

> Anyone planning to compile a similar reference work should have a good physical constitution and a thick skin. Dictionary making means organizing, remembering, anticipating, supervising, writing, rewriting, doublechecking, cajoling, soothing, encouraging, justifying, and a host of other "ings". A miracle perhaps, but during either term of preparation, none of our core staff lost time due to illness, not even nervous breakdowns [in the face of provocative issues, lack of money, final deadlines, and revision of articles under short deadlines].[26]

The process of editing an encyclopedia involves several steps that are roughly chronological in order but may overlap.[27] An early step is to campaign for the project itself—with funders, publishers, potential associate editors and article authors, and thought leaders in the relevant profession. This might take the form of formal presentations at professional meetings or discussions with various professional committees, funding agencies, and publisher representatives.[28] One of the topics that might be covered in these discussions is why an encyclopedia is the right tool, as opposed for example, to a textbook, handbook, or a reviewing journal or series of essays that review the field.[29] The next step is to identify the senior editorial staff who will lead most of the daily activities in the creation of the encyclopedia and an editorial board to advise on these activities. On larger encyclopedias, there might be a third group of associate editors, each one with overall responsibility for a particular subdiscipline

---

[23] Fenske 2010, p. 58.

[24] Fenske 2010.

[25] Fenske 2010, p. 60.

[26] Kallman 1994, p. 18.

[27] As Kallman 1994, p. 6, notes, the editors are working on two fronts, simultaneously intellectual and practical: "...the editor had to plan on two fronts: the intellectual concept and its practical realization. On the first, it was necessary to define scope, audience, style, degree of comprehensiveness and scale of detail. On the practical side it was necessary to enlist staff, contributors and advisors, to estimate workloads and target dates, to design workflow patterns, to equip offices and to write contracts and reports."

[28] See Fenske 2010 on Peuckert's efforts to campaign for his encyclopedia.

[29] See Sutton 1962 about these start-up issues. On the difference between an encyclopedia and a textbook, see Ashmore 1962, p. 15.

covered by the encyclopedia. These associate editors would "have more duties than an advisory editor but considerably fewer than a full-time editor."[30]

Perhaps the most satisfying intellectual part of the encyclopedia writing process is to identify the field that is to be covered by the encyclopedia, define its boundaries, and break it down into a list of "right-sized" topics that cover all the relevant material.[31] In a field that is studied by multiple academic subdisciplines—such as computer science, which is studied by mathematicians, engineers, and in the case of human–computer interaction by psychologists and designers—there may be disagreements about the unity of knowledge or the boundaries of the field.[32] On the other hand, if the editorial staff is small and the lead editor is strong-willed, the organization of knowledge may be primarily a reflection of that one person's view of the field.[33] It is often not easy to come to consensus about which topics to include in an encyclopedia. Here is one simple example faced by the editors of the Canadian music encyclopedia: "Some vexing problems had to be faced. If one proposed ten clarinetists for inclusion, for sure someone would assert "I know at least three who are as good or better." If one included 13, the same would happen again until there were 20 or 30."[34] Some topics need to be covered because they are so ever-present at the time the encyclopedia is being created; for example, it would be impossible to think of creating an encyclopedia of computer science in 2025 without extensive coverage of artificial intelligence and large language models. But for other topics, the inclusion decision is most satisfactorily made by applying a synthetic conception of the knowledge to be covered in the encyclopedia.[35]

Next comes the more tedious task of matching topics with potential authors, convincing these authors to sign on to write the articles, and negotiating with the author about what is to be and not to be covered in the article. Sills explains that for

---

[30] Sills 1969, pp. 1170-71. Sills describes how the advisory board interacted with the editors on the writing of the social science encyclopedia he has studied.

[31] As Kallman 1994 (p. 8) describes the process of filling out the list of topics: "After defining the scope and approach, the most urgent task was to decide 'who and what' were 'in and out'. The list of entries is the very backbone of encyclopedia preparation. Its compilation is the greatest fun-and the greatest headache. It evokes a sense of power, the joy of discovery, and a foretaste of what should be said in this or that article, but above all, it instills responsibility for fairness."

Couch 1962 (p. 21) discusses the value of having a synthetic principle for organizing, arranging, and classifying material in an encyclopedia.

However, as Van Doren 1962 (p. 23) notes, this process of creating the intellectual boundaries for an encyclopedia are not always clear cut; or, as he stated, "Most encyclopedias... grow; they are not created." Sills 1969, p. 1172, made a similar point of fine tuning the encyclopedia's goal during the first couple of years of work on the project.

[32] See France 1998 on how these issues of disciplinary attitudes, interdisciplinary writing, and unity of knowledge beliefs played out in eighteenth- and nineteenth-century encyclopedias.

[33] Fenske 2010 has discussed how the legend encyclopedia was primarily a reflection of the lead editor Peuckert.

[34] Kallman 1994, p. 9.

[35] See Van Doren 1962 (p. 24) on reasons for including a topic in an encyclopedia. In some cases, this synthetic principle is attained by discussion and consensus-reaching by the scholars in the relevant subject areas, See, Sills 1962, p. 32, on this topic.

the social science encyclopedia, the editors "consulted textbooks, abstract journals, and colleagues, to make sure that no important topic was overlooked [and for building lists of potential contributors]."[36] Often, there was a mismatch between potential authors and topics the editors had that needed to be covered, as Kallman explains about the Canadian music encyclopedia:

> Somehow we found our contributors—and they found us—often after laborious detours of mismatching writer and subject, or misreading good intentions for ability to deliver. They were a motley crowd of academics, folk music collectors, local historians, music journalists, broadcasters, librarians, orchestra committee members, freelance music researchers (usually recent graduates), and many others. Some had thorough knowledge of a single subject [that they had personal connection to]—while others knew how to assemble information about people and organizations they had never heard of. Some wrote only one article, others several dozens. Some knew how to write but not how to explore and assess sources, others knew their field but were poor writers. Few articles had to be rejected, but many were rewritten by [the encyclopedia's] staff. Even the best contributions required such adjustments as adaptation to house style, excision of material treated in related entries, or addition of current information.[37]

Even after these questions about topics and authors were largely resolved, there were numerous ongoing tasks faced by the editors. A clear and comprehensive set of instructions to contributors needed to be written and distributed. These established house style and led to greater coherence across articles.[38] The editors had to interact with the authors once their draft articles were submitted. As Kallman explained about the encyclopedia he studied:

> [I]deally writers should see the edited version of their assignment. Indeed, we followed this when major changes had been made or pieces were highly technical. However, under the pressure of time, routine changes could not always be submitted to the author. To protect the legal entity responsible for the project [there was a legal disclaimer].[39]

The editors also had to interact with the individuals and organizations written about in the encyclopedia:

> It is even more questionable whether subjects should see the proposed text for their entry. In cases of doubtful or missing information, it is wise to do this in a controlled situation, e.g. by telephone, quoting only essential passages? Such checking can eradicate innocent errors. But submitting an entire article for approval might provoke entanglement with egos and cost precious time in argument.[40]

Moreover, as the encyclopedia scholar DeGrazia notes, the editors faced a seemingly endless set of editorial details:

---

[36] Sills 1969, p. 1171. The social science encyclopedia drew mainly upon active researchers to draft articles and serve on the advisory board; some were department heads or directors of research institutes, but some were more junior scholars. (Sills 1969, p. 1171).

[37] Kallman 1994, p. 11.

[38] See Kallman 1994 (p. 12) on instructions to contributors.

[39] Kallman 1994, p. 12.

[40] Kallman 1994, p. 12.

Thereupon encyclopedism becomes a series of committee meetings over alphabetism vs. topic headings, writing down vs. writing up, historicism vs. contemporaneity, group writing vs. individual contributions, five million words vs. ten million, illustrations vs. text, bound books vs. contrivances other than books, national vs. world references, how much art "exists" vs. how much science "exists," and information vs. exhortation. All of these are what I should call the important questions for executive decisions, but not the primary decisions of encyclopedism.[41]

The process may also involve ongoing interaction between the editors and the article authors, as Kallman explains:

All editors read every article, the associate editor all those in his realm. We would identify doubtful or duplicated information, note obvious gaps, do instant corrections, compare impressions and sometimes return the article to the author or the staff for further work. If changes were substantial, a second or third reading would take place before final approval. The style editors were largely occupied with applying abbreviations, spellings, and formulas for the "banners" of biographies. They might divide long sentences, improve awkward phrasing, and eradicate inconsistencies, contradictions, and anachronisms. It is amazing how many pairs of eyes it can take to spot obvious errors.[42]

Modern digital tools have made the life of the encyclopedia editor easier, if not easy. Before online meetings, it was difficult and expensive to convene the editorial staff if it was spread across a large nation.[43] In preparing the first volume of his encyclopedia, Peukert prepared 750,000 index cards.[44] The editors needed to mark up data, do fact-checking, and create metadata as part of the publication process—all of which was simplified by electronic files.[45]

5.2 ECS Editorial Process

The production of the ECS was a leaner operation than that of many other encyclopedias we have discussed. Ralston was the sole editor of the first edition, although he had an assistant. Reilly joined him for the next two, and with Hemmendinger, the fourth edition had three editors. The third edition also had a managing editor, who worked with Ralston on *Abacus*, a magazine that he edited for five years in the 1980s.[46] Hemmendinger, who had primary responsibility for the fourth edition, had an administrative assistant for the first year, whose main role was to maintain a database of article status and handle routine correspondence with authors. The

---

[41] DeGrazia 1962, p. 40; as Sills 1969 noted (p. 1171), another task for the editors was to "recommend replacement authors for articles that did not appear or were unsatisfactory."

[42] Kallman 1994, pp. 12-13.

[43] Kallman 1994, p. 5.

[44] Fenske 2010.

[45] See Kallman 1994, pp. 13-15, on markup and metadata. On the importance of metrics to an encyclopedia, see Stvilia et al. 2005.

[46] Lee, J. A. N. *Computer Pioneers*, online edition, https://history.computer.org/pioneers/ralston.html. accessed May 4, 2025.

publisher had a staff member who managed articles and record-keeping at their end. The editors conferred regularly by email, often daily, and held day-long meetings several times a year, when Ralston, then living in London, visited the United States.

When work on the fourth edition began, the editors met to review all the third-edition articles. There were several categories: replace, major revision, minor revision, unchanged, or delete. Articles not needing change were generally short ones on well-defined topics, and those to be deleted were on topics that once seemed important but no longer seemed so. Many of the remaining articles needed either minor or major changes, and those to be replaced were poorly written or were on topics that needed quite different treatment. A look back through the editions shows that not only did articles become dated and so were dropped, for example, "acoustic coupler" (for modems) and "computing center", but some topics that should have been included were not. Articles on two basic topics in programming language implementation, "activation record" and "compiler", for example, were not added until the third edition, though they could well have been in the first.

In addition to exercising their own judgment, the editors commissioned 25 reviews of each of the nine sections of the ECS, with some divided among several reviewers. The publisher's budget that had gone to the editorial board of previous editions went to reviewer honoraria. Reviewers were asked for a narrative account of strengths and weaknesses of their areas, a rating of each article as good, acceptable, or unacceptable, with recommendations for revision or deletion, and suggestions of new articles with possible authors. All but three reviews were completed; the section on the mathematics of computing was the only one with no review, but since it was Ralston's field, the omission was not a major problem. Six reviewers were third-edition authors, and six others became authors for the fourth edition. The reviews were generally well-done, and some were quite excellent; Ralston remarked on their high quality and said that he thought that the editors got much more for their money than from the earlier editorial boards.[47] Several reviews suggested extensive reorganization of their areas, particularly those that had grown by accretion over the course of several editions. While these suggestions had merit, in most cases the editors decided against such wholesale revision because of the considerable labor it would require, involving coordination among many authors.

Some authors of fourth-edition articles had been with the ECS from the start, many of them found through Ralston's ACM connections, and several of them wrote ten or more articles. If an existing author was unable to revise an article that needed work, the editors often did the revision themselves if the article was basically sound; in other cases, a new author revised it or wrote an entirely new article. When the editors decided on new articles, they sought potential authors among those suggested by reviewers, those with whom an editor was acquainted or knew by reputation, and in some cases, by getting further advice and suggestions from colleagues. Having chosen authors, they sent invitation letters, which included the publisher's guidelines for article format, references style, and so forth, and described what the editors wanted:

---

[47] Email to Hemmendinger, November 12, 1995.

5.2 ECS Editorial Process

> Let me emphasize that your audience will include both computer scientists and laypeople such as bright secondary-school students. Our contributors will need to provide a level of scholarship acceptable to their peers as well as the clarity of exposition appropriate to a layperson.
>
> Personal viewpoints will be acceptable in your article; however, grinding of personal axes will not. Please do not hesitate to suggest topics related to those on which you will be writing, as well as those that you believe deserve a separate article. Feel free to suggest topics that we have not considered.

The editors tried to ensure that articles met these rather elementary requirements, and they revised articles that did not initially meet them, but they did not strive for stylistic unity across articles. They rejected only a few articles; when they did reject an article and could not readily find a new author, one of the editors sometimes wrote it. For the 4th edition, Ralston wrote 13 articles, Reilly 49, and Hemmendinger 16. Although the editors had no explicit division of labor, most of Ralston's articles concerned mathematical topics, Reilly's covered terms commonly encountered by computer users such as "password" and "wizard"—often brief—and Hemmendinger's focused on programming languages and computer architecture. Overall, however, the ECS did not strongly reflect the editors' views.

The letter to authors added that the editors expected there would be electronic forms of the fourth edition, at least a CD-ROM and a World Wide Web version. This expectation turned out to be aspirational, as we discuss below.

When work began on the first ECS edition, network email was new and restricted to the few institutions on the Arpanet. The Internet had just started in 1983, when the second edition appeared. When the third edition was published in 1993, email had become more common, but the World Wide Web and the Mosaic browser had just appeared. When work on the fourth edition started in mid-1995, several browsers and search engines were available, and the editors used them heavily to track down authors, who had often moved to new positions since the last edition. Particularly during the final stages of production, Web browsers also helped in fact-checking and in tracking down missing details of reference citations. The AltaVista search engine, introduced in 1995, was one of the most useful tools for finding author addresses and for searching for material for articles. By 1998, the editors were largely using Google instead, although most of the work was done by then. With only a few exceptions, nearly all interaction with authors was through email. That included communicating editorial changes, and the editors were careful to consult authors about all of their proposed revisions. Given the timing with which these Internet tools became available, the production of the ECS depended much more heavily on them than previous encyclopedia work had been able to do.

Many of the editorial tasks were no different from those for other encyclopedias, but one issue was specific to computer science: Articles had examples of computer programs, and it was important that they be correct. In addition to trying to ensure that they implemented their algorithm correctly, it was remarkable how readily program text could become corrupted in the process of inserting it into an article, or as a result of subsequent editing that was not intended to affect the program code. It is all too easy to change one piece of text and find that the change unintentionally changed another part as well. The most reliable way to ensure correct program code was not to insert a working program into an article, but rather to extract it from the article at the end of the editing process, compile it to machine code, and run it to be sure that it still worked and was apparently correct. When the editors did this with programs from old articles as well as from new ones, a number of errors showed up, both in program logic and in program text; and these errors had to be corrected.

Another low-level editorial task was handling the format of third-edition articles. As Ralston described in his *Annals* article, the fourth edition started with a new publisher, International Thomson. It had received the third-edition articles from Van Nostrand in the Ventura desktop-publishing format.[48] Although Ventura could convert its format to those of word processors such as Microsoft Word, Thomson apparently did not have the Ventura program itself and just gave the editors the old articles in Ventura format. As the editors needed to provide those articles to authors, who would revise them. Hemmendinger wrote some programs in a scripting language to convert basic Ventura to the RTF format for Word, plain text, or LaTeX; they could handle most text font styles and special characters, though not tables or complex mathematical notation.

The publisher provided a style guide that addressed issues such as reference formatting, article structure, spelling, and abbreviations; the editors added advice about article level and content. We do not have information about the process of editing submissions for the first three editions. Many fourth-edition authors used Word, while some used LaTeX, and a few wrote unformatted text or marked up tearsheets. The editors used the Word revision tool extensively to correspond with authors about changes and marked up LaTeX article with comments, and at least two of the three editors read each article. The editorial assistant, who helped for the first year, maintained records of due dates and article status; the publisher maintained these later.

The outcome of the editorial work was that the fourth edition had 623 articles written by over 450 authors, compared to 470 and 210 in the first edition. There were 103 new articles (about 20%), 160 extensively revised, some 250 with minor or no revision, 75 deleted, and 35 merged with other articles. The majority of authors were from the United States, with nearly 20% from other countries, with the United Kingdom, Canada, France, Germany most heavily represented. Roughly 75% of authors were at universities or colleges, and 25% worked at companies.

---

[48] As Ventura was introduced only in 1986 and was not commonly used aside from desktop publishing, Van Nostrand must have converted what third-edition authors provided into Ventura.

Chapter 6
Funding and Publishing

Abstract This chapter discusses issues of funding and publishing in writing an encyclopedia generally and in particular for the *Encyclopedia of Computer Science*. Topics include finding the financing from a professional organization, foundation, or government agency; speaking publicly to sell the idea of the project and market the final result; and identifying an appropriate publisher and working with them.

6.1 Encyclopedia Scholars on Funding and Publishing

In the twentieth century, it was generally expensive to produce an encyclopedia.[1] Some of the multivolume encyclopedias for the general public, such as *Funk & Wagnalls* or *Britannica*, were funded by the purchase of copies, often on a subscription model.[2] But for specialty encyclopedias, it was often too large a financial commitment for either the editor or the publisher to cover the sizable up-front costs. In these cases, it was more common for the editor or the publisher to obtain a grant from a foundation or a professional society to create, publish, and distribute the encyclopedia.[3] In this section, we will cover two topics, the funding of the modern encyclopedia and its publication (including distribution).

The idea for a specialized encyclopedia often originated with an established member of the relevant academic profession, or from a conversation in a professional committee meeting or at a professional conference. Once a decision was made to seek an encyclopedia project, there was often a campaign to consolidate interest within the professional community and to find funding. This might involve the prospective editor giving a series of lectures about the proposed project at distinguished universities, making formal presentations to the relevant professional societies, or visiting various potential funders which might include government agencies, professional

---

[1] While the scale and expense of most encyclopedias was much smaller, in 1963 *Encyclopaedia Britannica* employed more than 200 staff members and cost more than $3 million annually. (Ashmore).

[2] Ashmore 1962, p. 16.

[3] Fenske 2010.

societies, leading companies in related business areas, publishers, or occasionally wealthy individuals.

There was significant value added to the editor by working with an established publisher, as Kallman explains from his work on the Canadian music encyclopedia:

> In addition to devising proper business and editorial structures, early liaison with a publisher was invaluable for the firm's experience with marketing, pricing, production scheduling, and readers' requirements. Familiarity with house style (e.g., spellings, abbreviations, and manuscript format) saved hours of time wasted on avoidable correcting.[4]

Public relations was also a significant concern, especially in the case where the encyclopedia is costly. As the encyclopedia scholar Michaela Fenske observed, "Creating a suitable narrative for the public was thus important. In this sense, the marketing of academic products does not differ from that of other goods, be it a brand of automobile or a soft drink: the success and the acceptance of any product is also a result of clever advertising."[5]

Most academics who write or edit a book contribute in a minor way to the marketing of the product. They might present a talk about the book at one or two professional meetings, for example. In today's world, there are additional marketing opportunities, such as lecture tours, podcasts, blogs, and postings to online mailing lists and social media sites; but only a minority of academics take these extra efforts. They tend to rely on the publisher for their publicity.[6]

The publisher of the specialized encyclopedia, such as one for computer science, had two principal markets: sales to libraries and individual sales. The major publishers already had well-established connections to librarians and could market effectively there. Marketing to individuals usually took the form of displays at professional conferences, fall and spring book catalogs once mailed and more recently distributed online, and the occasional flyer for an individual book or series of books.

Encyclopedias were often good investments for publishers,[7] and it was not uncommon to find a technical publisher establishing its own encyclopedia project for the subject areas in which it was most active. Thus, it was not particularly challenging for a prospective specialty encyclopedia author to find an interested publisher. This proclivity for publishing grand reference works seems to have increased in recent years:

---

[4] Kallman 1994, p. 5.

[5] Fenske 2010 (citation in original text removed), p. 66.

[6] Peuckert, with his legends encyclopedia, was an unusually active self-promoter: "Institutionalization is also a question of communication. As authoritative formats, encyclopedias require a serious habitus: thus, Peuckert asked his publisher for stationery and postcards bearing the project's letterhead and special paper for manuscript. However, Peuckert's enormous appetite for such supplies was surprising to the publisher. But Peuckert was quite experienced in public relations, and he used these materials to network with the media, working to advertise his project in the most important public medium of the day: the radio. Creating a publicly available narrative about the legend encyclopedia and its history was an essential part of developing it as an institution...." (Fenske 2010, p. 66)

[7] Fenske 2010.

Today new reference works, especially multivolume encyclopedias and dictionaries, owe more to the economic rhythms of the publishing industry, as it competes for mass markets and copes with higher educational costs and government taxes, than to new accumulations of knowledge.[8]

But the experienced publisher would want to shape the project to ensure its marketability. As one encyclopedia historian observed:

> The first edition of the *Britannica* displays a noticeable lack of interest in grand schemes of classification. No doubt this partly reflected the practical, business-like attitude of its editors and publishers: William Smellie, Colin Macfarquhuar, and James Tytler. These men were interested in science, but they were not *philosophes* concerned with reorganizing the intellectual world.[9]

Another important element of the publishing ecosystem was the bookseller. "Booksellers were primarily concerned to make a profit and to sell their products, and consequently they sought out first and foremost those works that were of interest to the largest possible number of their contemporaries.... Contemporary lexicographers agree that dictionaries are made to be sold."[10]

6.2 ECS Funding and Publishing

Ralston's article on the ECS editions describes its eight publishers.[11] Petrocelli/Charter acquired the first edition from Auerbach Publishers; Van Nostrand Reinhold had acquired it from Petrocelli for the second edition and also published the first printing of the third edition before transferring its computing books to International Thomson Computer Press (ITCP), a subsidiary, with which the fourth-edition editors drew up a contract in late 1995. Two years later, ITCP transferred the ECS to International Thomson Business Press (London), which sold it to U.K. Macmillan Reference, part of the Macmillan Group, in mid-1998. By the time that the book appeared in 2000, the Nature Publishing Group had acquired Macmillan Reference and then sold it to Wiley & Sons (U.K.) in 2003, so that the first printing had the imprint of Grove Reference, a division of Nature Publishing, but the next had that of John Wiley & Sons.

The budget in the ITCP contract was what the editors proposed. As the "Actual" column of Table 6.1 shows, their estimates were fairly inaccurate. The administrative assistant for Hemmendinger worked primarily on the initial stages, maintaining a database of article status and their authors, and the task occupied a little more than the first year of editorial work. As nearly all author correspondence was by email and material was submitted online, postage and paper costs were minimal. Reviewing

---

[8] Sullivan 1990, p. 333.
[9] Yeo 1991, p. 29.
[10] Menagarishvili 2012, p. 22.
[11] Ralston 2004.

Table 6.1 *Encyclopedia of computer science*, fourth-edition budget

Category	Budgeted	Actual
Administrative assistant	$17,500	$2800
Postage, telephone, copying, travel	7000	1000
Reviews of the third edition	9000	6150
Computing hardware for editors	9000	< 9000
Author payments	15,000	30,000
Total	$57,500	< $48,950

cost less than budgeted because several reviews were not submitted. The computing hardware included a personal computer for Hemmendinger,[12] who did the bulk of the editorial work, and it cost about half of the amount budgeted for hardware (Table 6.1).

Author payments for new articles were calculated at 8 cents/word, and honoraria for revisions were fixed amounts that depended on their extent. The budgeted amount was a guess made before the editors decided on the number of new articles or on the extent of revision, and as a result of their getting more new ones and more extensive revisions than anticipated, the amount grew considerably. Authors of new and most revised articles were also to be given a copy of the book, though the budget does not reflect that cost. If the publisher's marginal production cost of a volume was 10% of the initial $150 list price, this added about $5000 for about 340 volumes, bringing the actual total close to the budgeted total.[13] By contrast, first-edition authors were offered 2 cents/word and a 50% discount on purchase of the book. According to Ralston,[14] Van Nostrand had suggested the more generous book offer to third-edition authors, and he proposed the same for the fourth edition (Macmillan, which had not drawn up the original contract, did not like the complimentary book offer but honored it).

ITCP provided the editors with the third-edition articles, either in the Ventura desktop-publishing format or as Microsoft Word files. Most graphics had to be scanned from pages. The publisher provided the usual guidelines for formatting references, spelling, abbreviations, and so forth. Although it would accept article submissions as either Word or TeX files, it was not well-prepared to handle the latter and asked for printed copy as well. This was a significant defect for a book whose authors were computer scientists, many of whom preferred the LaTeX version of TeX, particularly for mathematical notation.

---

[12] For the obligatory note about computer costs back then: the computer supplied to Hemmendinger was a high-end 133 MHz Pentium system that ran Windows 95. It had 16 MB of main memory, a large (1.2 GB) hard drive, a 28 Kbps modem, an ethernet card, and included Microsoft Office Professional and Encarta. The price was $4106.

[13] The 10% estimate for the cost of paper, printing, and binding was the editors' initial rough estimate, supported now by an informed opinion on a web page: www.quora.com/How-much-percentage-of-a-books-listed-price-does-it-account-for-marginal-cost (accessed January 26, 2025).

[14] Email to Hemmendinger, May 20, 1996.

6.2 ECS Funding and Publishing

The ITCP editor who worked with the ECS editors was particularly interested in having articles on computing applications. The ECS did have a number of these articles and resisted—generally successfully—the ITCP effort to add more on topics that they thought were narrow or likely to be short-lived. Another contentious issue was the ITCP desire to have formal contributor agreements. Ralston argued that he had not had them for the previous editions and that they were an unnecessary burden. He was eventually willing to accept them even though by then the editors had lined up many new or repeat authors, but the multiple changes in publisher meant that none of them actually produced the forms, and the fourth edition appeared without contributor agreements. When Wiley began planning for a fifth edition, which, as we discuss in Chap. 7, never materialized, it did send out written agreement forms, which about a fourth of current authors returned.

The ECS editors were diligent, however, in obtaining permissions to use or reuse images. The publisher held the copyright to articles by default, although a few authors asked to retain it, to which the publisher agreed, subject to its having a nonexclusive right to use an author's article. The article by Richard Stallman on the Free Software Foundation had its "copyleft" agreement attached to it.

The publisher marketed the ECS through ads in professional scientific and library journals. A mid-2000 report lists ads in *Scientific American, Communications of the ACM* [Association of Computing Machinery, one of two major computing professional organizations], *IEEE Computer* [IEEE Computer Society, the other organization], *Library Journal,* and *Today's Librarian,* as well as in publisher ads that included ECS among other titles. Publisher exhibits at professional and library conferences included the ECS, and the publisher also sent direct mail to university, technical highschool, and public libraries (we do not have a count), and to members of the ACM and IEEE Computer Society. The direct mail offered a $125 discounted price, which was also on the Grove Dictionaries web page for at least two years. As well as these promotions in the United States, there were similar ones in the United Kingdom. At one point, the editors urged additional ads in popular computing magazines, but the publisher balked at the $43,000 fee for an ad in *PC Computing* despite the evident virtues of the ECS.

We have reports on ECS sales in the first years. Macmillan reported that at the end of 2000, a few months after publication, university libraries had bought 270 copies, public libraries 151, high schools 34, and individuals 81. Wholesalers and retailers had taken 1800 copies, 80% of them by Baker & Taylor and Ingram; the former sold largely to libraries and the latter to retailers. Another report two years later was that nearly 5700 copies had sold. As Ralston reported in his *Annals* article,[15] that was about half of the number of sales of each of the first three editions. He speculated that the 50% increase over the price of the third edition was an impediment, but another cause may have been the growing number of books available in print on all areas of computing. Yet another cause may have been the rise of online encyclopedias, which we discuss later.

---

[15] Ralston 2004, p. 43.

The $150 price of the fourth edition (later, $200) meant that most bookstores would not routinely stock it; and from the start, the editors were interested in having an abbreviated paperback version that mass-market bookstores would carry. Publishers expressed a similar interest, although ITCP initially proposed one that would have only the articles that focused on computer applications, rather than the comprehensive version that the editors wanted. The discussions that continued with International Thomson Business Press and then with Macmillan were about the editors' proposal, which solidified when Reilly agreed to edit it. He began work in 2001, after the fourth edition appeared, and completed most of that work in 2002. However, with the rapid turnover in publishers, it did not appear until 2004, under the Wiley imprint. While Wiley published many encyclopedias, those were primarily multivolume specialist sets intended for large libraries. It did not market the *Concise Encyclopedia of Computer Science*[16] effectively and failed to place it in the major mass-market bookstores. Also, since the articles from which it was derived were at least five years old, many had already become dated. At the time of this writing, the book has not sold enough copies to cover the royalty advance that the ECS editors received when work on it began.

It is unusual for an encyclopedia to go through so many publishers: twice as many as there were editions. The changes were not due to publishers' interest in the book, nor to relationships with the editors, but probably just a result of rapid changes in the publishing industry during the last part of the twentieth century. There was never any difficulty in finding the next publisher, as each turned over its list to the next. In fact, the editors of the fourth edition welcomed each change, as it appeared initially promising, though the promises were generally not borne out. The publishers were all helpful in production matters, and more knowledgeable about marketing than the editors were. The publishers did not contribute much to the content of the ECS, and the editors generally resisted their efforts to set a rigid timetable. The editors were disappointed, however, both in the failure to develop either a CD-ROM version of the book or an online version, despite initial discussions of each, and in the failure to market the concise edition effectively.

---

[16] Reilly 2004.

Chapter 7
Editions, Supplements, and Online Encyclopedias

Abstract This chapter discusses multiple editions, supplements, and online versions in writing an encyclopedia generally and in particular for the *Encyclopedia of Computer Science*. Topics include determining whether and when a new edition should be created, whether to create spinoff products such as annual issues with recent developments or a summary volume of top topics, and whether to add an online version and how it will relate to the print version.

7.1 Encyclopedia Scholars on Editions, Supplements, and Online Encyclopedias

With the ever-changing state of knowledge, there was an ongoing need to revise the material in an encyclopedia if it was to be kept up to date. With a print-form encyclopedia, there were two means to make these updates, periodic supplements to the main encyclopedia or a new edition of the encyclopedia. *Britannica*, for example, published an annual update, *The Book of the Year*.[1] The problem with supplements is that they needed to be made of a manageable size, so they typically included only the most important information appearing since the publication of the encyclopedia; and thus they could not accommodate the many additional changes that one might make to the entries in the encyclopedia, both in terms of new content or change in emphasis. In the case of a more specialized encyclopedia, the reason for change was not only new events but also new scholarship that provided a revised understanding of older events.[2]

---

[1] Ashmore 1962, p. 16.

[2] Kallman 1994, p. 18, explicitly states that the call for an updated Canadian music encyclopedia was new scholarship as well as new events. In writing about the decision to create a new edition of a scientific dictionary, Menagarishvili 2012 wrote what might be emphasized in the changes from one edition to the next: "In the case of *McGraw-Hill Dictionary of Scientific and Technical Terms*, which was published in the United States in the second half of the twentieth century and in the twenty-first century, the scientific knowledge economy in which the dictionary functioned can be described as progressive: creating each edition became a process that involved adding new knowledge as it developed. I also explain this by the cultural context: in the second half of the twentieth century, the

If there is an expectation that there will be updates to the original edition—whatever form they might take—it is important that plans be made to continue to collect data about errors in the original publication, new topics, new events, and new scholarship that might be relevant. For his folklore encyclopedia, Peuckert talked about institutionalizing the process, establishing routines, and retaining at least a small ongoing staff.[3] It was better not to have to start completely anew for each new supplement or edition.

The same stakeholders were at play in the decision to prepare a new edition as were involved in the decision to create the original edition. Did the editors of the previous edition have the drive to undertake a massive new edition? Did the community of scholars favor a new edition based on their judgments of both the quality and effectiveness of the earlier edition(s) and their views on how much material needed to be changed or added to the older edition(s)? How successful a venture was the previous edition for the publisher both financially and reputationally? Were funders such as foundations and professional societies convinced about the need for a new edition?

The creators of a subsequent edition had the advantage of much text that could be reused, a set of processes and individuals familiar with these processes, formal and informal reviews of the earlier editions to use as guides in making changes in the new edition, and some sense of the market (both size and characteristics of the most likely buying community) for the new edition.[4]

When there were multiple editions of an encyclopedia, there was often informal and sometimes formal discussion of which edition was best. Sometimes there is a consensus, e.g., about the superiority of the 11th (1911) edition of *Encyclopaedia Britannica*. Encyclopedia historian Harry Ashmore noted the devotedness to the particular edition readers grew up using:

> It is an aphorism of the trade that scholars tend to regard as the best in history the edition of an encyclopedia that preceded the current one. This is natural enough, I suppose. The defects of the set in hand are obvious, while the set first encountered in the dawn of intellectual discovery is bathed in the sentimental glow of selective memory.[5]

The existence of multiple editions of an encyclopedia encouraged the use of these various texts as the subject of academic scrutiny. One can follow the evolution of computer science over time by comparing and contrasting the content of the various editions of a computer science encyclopedia. Sills explained how one can undertake an intellectual history of an encyclopedia by "considering the path from the initial

---

development of science and technology was one of the most common themes, so adding smaller portions of information that was connected with the new developments rather than collecting all 'existing' knowledge became more widely spread."

[3] Fenske 2010.

[4] See Kallman 1994, p. 13, on these issues in the writing of a twentieth-century encyclopedia; Yeo 1991 on similar issues that came about in the writing of nineteenth-century encyclopedias.

[5] Ashmore 1962, p. 16.

table of contents to the published work."[6] Menagarishvili explains how one can use the sampling techniques of lexicographic archeology to compare editions:

> Lexicographic archaeology allowed me to compare different editions of the same dictionary in both cases. I copied every 20th page of the word list of the first edition of a dictionary for the analysis. Using every 20th page allowed me to analyze 5% of each dictionary. Because dictionaries tend to be rather voluminous and, therefore, difficult to analyze, this percentage was recommended for lexicographical studies by [Olga] Karpova in her "Introduction to Lexicography" course.[7]

Much has been written about the rise of online encyclopedias, such as Microsoft's Encarta, Wikipedia, and the change of *Encyclopaedia Britannica* to an online format (debuted in 1994, and since 2016 its only format).[8] For example, Encarta was Microsoft's effort to enter the encyclopedia business. It was published, first on CD-ROM and DVD, between 1993 and 2009. Wikipedia, founded in 2001 and still going strong today, was the first successful collaborative online encyclopedia. There were transitional forms, such as CD-ROMs, proprietary databases, and noninteractive copies of a print encyclopedia copied onto a Web site. Today there are both interactive online encyclopedias and powerful search engines, such as Google's, that make the entire Internet a place from which to retrieve information—and all are accessible through computer, tablet, cell phone, or any communication device that can be connected to the Internet.[9]

But it goes beyond our scope to tell the history of online encyclopedias. We are more interested here in how they changed the use and meaning of print encyclopedias and the concept of an encyclopedia itself. Even in electronic form, the underlying conception of an encyclopedia was as a book and among them as a source of expert knowledge that had been vetted and was therefore trustworthy.[10] With the passing of the print form of *Brittanica*, there was an increasing belief that the encyclopedia generally—but especially the print form—was both an antiquated material object and a reflection of a curious, old-fashioned idea that any single work could hold the key to knowledge. Nevertheless, historians and academic librarians continued to see the value of the printed encyclopedia, where the provenance of information was more certain than in open-source encyclopedias.[11] Whereas Wikipedia could be updated steadily, the economics of updating a print encyclopedia was measured

---

[6] Sills 1969, p. 1172.

[7] Menagarishvili 2012, p. 27.

[8] There is a large and growing literature about online encyclopedias. Some examples include O'Sullivan 2011; Roncaglia 2021; Rosenzweig 2006; Pang 1997; Flanagin & Metzger 2011; Tereszkiewicz, 2013; and Holman Rector 2008.

We find of particular interest the research by Shane Greenstein, his students, and his collaborators. See, for example, Greenstein 2012, 2017, 2019, 2024; Greenstein & Zhu 2012a, 2012b, 2014, 2016, 2018; Greenstein & Devereux 2017a, 2017b; Greenstein, Frazzano, and Meagher 2017; and Greenstein, Gu, and Zhu 2021.

[9] Ashmore 1962 discusses the important role of new technology in the evolving nature of the encyclopedia.

[10] Haider and Sundin 2014.

[11] See Wexelbaum 2012 on this point.

in years.[12] Print encyclopedias, especially those with a strong editorial hand, were careful about precision and standardization of the language, especially in comparison to open-source encyclopedias.[13]

7.2 ECS Editions, Supplements, and Online Versions

When Isaac Auerbach proposed a computer science encyclopedia in 1971, Ralston decided that the discipline was sufficiently well-defined to have one.[14] Nevertheless, the field changed rapidly, and several years after publication, the time seemed ready for a new edition. This remained true for the next three editions, each of which was produced about seven years after its predecessor (the third edition was delayed several years by an editor's health problems).

As a one-volume area encyclopedia, the ECS was always a small enterprise, different from major multivolume encyclopedias such as the *Encyclopaedia Britannica* or specialist sets that were bought only by libraries. ECS had at first only one, and later only several editors and no more than one staff member. Continuity resulted from the editorial membership's changing only by accretion, so that the original purpose, to provide a view or snapshot of the state of the field, did not change significantly. The editors decided when to start a new edition, without external impetus such as a publisher or advisory board review might have provided. This process had the merit, at least from the editors' perspective, of there being few constraints on their work, and perhaps the demerit of there being no institutional process and few external influences apart from the editorial board of the first three editions and the reviewers who evaluated the third-edition articles in preparation for the fourth edition. The editors believed that this process worked well.

Successive editions added articles on new topics, dropped some outdated ones, made minor or major changes to others, but generally did not reorganize them significantly. By the fourth edition, the editors did reorganize some groups of articles, although not as much as might have been appropriate, either because of their wanting to retain articles by important authors, or because of the extensive labor that would be required, including needing to get groups of authors to collaborate in repartitioning topics. Despite this limited revision structure, the ECS continued to be a reasonably accurate view of the field and of major applications of computing; if it missed some trends that were becoming important, it also avoided following enthusiasms that did not last.

The view of the field that the ECS editions offered also showed a changing understanding of what was essential to the field and what was inessential, being unfamiliar rather than actually novel. The first two editions had an entry for "Key," the element

---

[12] See Sutton 1962 on this point.

[13] Menagarishvili 2012 discusses this point with respect to dictionaries; an analogous point can be made about encyclopedias.

[14] Ralston 2004, p. 42.

of a data object by means of which the object was looked up in a table or put into a sorted order of such objects. Although the term may have been unfamiliar, the activity was not, and including an article on it was more about vocabulary than substance. Other first-edition articles were on "Cursor," "Intelligent Terminal," and "Decrement," which also were later dropped as inessential; their early presence reflected the relative unfamiliarity of computers and their terminology.[15]

We review the changes in the ECS editions treatments of two topics to get an idea of how its view of the field developed. Computer networking underwent substantial changes in the last quarter of the twentieth century—both in its technology and in its economic and social importance—and so we look at the ECS articles on networks and on computing in society across the four editions.

The Computer Networks article in the first two editions describes several sorts of connection: remote terminals connected to a single computer, remote computers whose output was carried by messenger to a central one (now sometimes called "sneakernet"—in one case, via roller skates[16]), a central computer that used specialized computers for services, and independent computers that shared program or data resources. The article notes that the last is becoming the primary meaning of "network" and refers to the Arpanet as well as other early networks. The article takes a relatively low-level view, discussing components and basic configurations. The fourth-edition article also addresses these topics, but it takes a higher-level view, discussing network architecture, applications, major examples of networks, and plans for advanced networks.

The Data Communications article shows similar evolution. In the first two editions, it was divided into two sections: principles and software. The former described the physical conditions of signal transmission and its implications for coding, and the article continued to address those topics in the last two editions, although with more attention to public networking. The software sections in the early editions addressed quite low-level details of program logic. Once again, the third edition had a higher-level account of the software; it added a third section, on communication standards. The fourth edition dropped the software section, although other articles covered some of its topics, expanded the standards section moderately, and mentioned the growing

---

[15] One might study ECS by examining the individual articles. Since there are so many, one might wish to take a sampling approach. If one were to conduct an archaeological analysis of the ECS editions, as Menagarishvili 2012 described in her dissertation on science dictionaries, where she analyzed 5% (every 20th page) of dictionaries, one would have to make a more sparing selection or analyze 100 pages of the 2000-page ECS fourth edition. One strategy could be to select an article every 30 pages of the 1500-page first edition (50 selections) and trace their history though the editions to look at their revisions, incorporation into other articles, or abandonment. We have not done this, however, because we question whether the knowledge gained is worth the effort. But if we had, the first few selections to study would be: Access methods, Administrative business applications, Analog computers, Arithmetic computer, Assemblers, Automation, Boolean algebra, Codes, Computational complexity, and Computer-assisted learning and teaching.

[16] In an IEEE oral history, Joyce Currie Little described carrying data this way through a long Convair Aircraft building, from an IBM 650 to a wind tunnel whose operators used its output: https://ethw.org/Oral-History:Joyce_Little.

interest in distributed computing, which had its own article, triple the length of the third-edition one.

User-level network services were not addressed in the first edition. The second edition included a number of references to electronic mail, e.g., in articles on office automation and on time sharing and mentions its early start with the Arpanet. It was covered an article in the third edition, with cross-references to articles on bulletin boards, conferencing, and local area networks. The fourth edition had a much-expanded article, along with new articles on the Internet and on the World Wide Web. Several third-edition articles referred to the Internet, but we should keep in mind that the Internet did not receive much popular use until the early 1990s; for example, America Online became available for Microsoft Windows in 1991.

The first-edition article on Computers and Society (by Calvin Gotlieb), our second topic for comparison, starts by saying that any application of computers in the public sector could illustrate their effects and cautions about risks of data collection. It addresses three main topics: effects on employment, on individuals, and on organizations and politics. In each, the approach is to treat computing as novel, with effects yet to be understood. The first describes the effects of earlier automation on the composition of the work force and anticipates similar ones, though it is agnostic about whether the introduction of computing will increase or decrease skill requirements. Overall, the article describes the possible effects of computers as sufficiently new that they cannot yet be fully assessed: they can accumulate more information about individuals than was possible earlier, with concomitant risks and benefits. Similarly, their effects on the balance of power in organizations were mentioned, e.g., shifting from centralizing information and power to decentralizing and redistributing it, but it was deemed too early to know how that might change institutional and political values and goals.

The second edition article was renamed Computing and Society, perhaps to emphasize the activity rather than the machines. Its author, Rob Kling, worked on ethics and societal issues, and the article has a new section on social impacts. It discusses quality-of-life issues: possible dependency on technology and the problems of complexity in large systems; it refers to E. M. Forster's story *The Machine Stops*.[17] It discusses possible effects on moral behavior, e.g., by enabling computer crime, on the consolidation of power among those who already hold it, and on communication. All are potentially far-reaching, and all too early to provide a complete assessment.

The third-edition article, entitled Computers in Society, written by Eric Roberts, a computer science educator, has a new orientation: computers have become ubiquitous, and government, businesses, and science all depend on them. Such dependency brings risks of failure of increasingly complex systems and risks of success—transformations of work, invasions of privacy, and reliance on computer data collection and manipulation. Unlike the earlier articles, this one devotes considerable space to problems of reliability, software failure, and malicious uses of computing. In addition to risks due to failure, computing has a major effect on society when it works as intended. The fourth-edition article by the same author is not significantly different.

---

[17] Forster 1909.

7.2 ECS Editions, Supplements, and Online Versions

In both examples of changes across editions, the earlier versions pay more attention to computers themselves—what they do and how they do it. As computation becomes more familiar to readers, they pay more attention to matters of policy—decisions about what computation *should* do rather than how the computation is done. While all four editions cover technical aspects of computing thoroughly in many articles, overall, each edition pays more attention to the nontechnical aspects than did the previous one.

In addition to the concise edition mentioned in Chap. 6, which was an attempt to reach a broader audience, rather than a supplementary work, the editors of the fourth edition planned several "companion" volumes that would include some ECS articles together with more specialized ones. Their areas were communication and networking, computer graphics, and (at the suggestion of the ITCP editor) one on computing applications. Although they had a prospective editor for the first, broader volume, in the end it did not materialize, and only the computer graphics companion volume was eventually published. It was not very successful, and there were no more such companions, although a major reason was the multiple changes in publisher.

The editors expected to have digital versions of the ECS: at least a CD-ROM that would accompany the volume and perhaps be sold separately, also an online version. They discussed their expectations with ITCP when it became the publisher; they were interested, though like the editors, without much experience. Discussions included having an appropriately indexed CD-ROM, perhaps with the Netscape Web browser for reading it. They also considered putting the CD-ROM contents online, probably to be available by subscription; throughout the discussions between the editors and ITCP, the latter wanted to be sure that there was a manageable way to produce income, and it was not clear how to do that.

One proposal by the editors was to start by putting the third-edition articles on a free Web site as the third edition was no longer a source of income, to be a way to build interest in a subsequent fourth-edition site. A sticking point was the publisher's lack of experience in converting the text, either existing or new, to HTML, although there were companies that could do it. ITCP was also interested in making a Web version that could be continuously revised and updated, perhaps with a print edition to appear at intervals. It was never clear, though, how such maintenance would be managed, as authors were not likely to take on the work for probably quite modest pay, and the publisher was not up to the task. The editors did not address this issue, but their invitation letter to potential authors said that there would certainly be a CD-ROM and that they planned a Web version that might become the center of a larger computing database. Although preliminary, they suggested that authors keep in mind how their article might become hypertext. Discussions continued for a while, but neither ITCP nor its successor publishers ever got to the point of producing either a CD-ROM or an online version—a major disappointment to the editors. This was also a missed opportunity, although it was never clear how to charge for an online edition.

Although the publisher did not succeed in producing an online version, in 2010, the ACM Digital Library added the ECS, making all of its articles and appendices available for download. As of July 2025, there had been 316,726 downloads. Forty

Table 7.1 Most frequently downloaded articles, with the number of downloads

Arithmetic-logic unit	14,855	Sequential machine	1778
Computational complexity	8522	Information retrieval	1750
Natural language processing	6438	Access methods	1619
Digital computers, history of	5252	User interface	1449
Abstract data type	4445	Programming language standards	1391
Object-oriented analysis and design	4376	Optical character recognition	1375
Interactive input devices	4044	Executable statement	1358
Guarded command	3860	Instruction decoding	1338
Backus-Naur form	3267	Bit slicing	1284
Artificial intelligence	3193	Cyclic redundancy check	1273
Machine learning	2976	Cache memory	1244
IBM system 360/370/390 series	2939	Multiprogramming	1244
Perceptron	2758	Procedure-oriented languages	1213
Flowchart	2730	Algol 68	1174
Input–output control system	2693	Index register	1093
Client–server computing	2624	Analog computer	1051
Electronic commerce	2566	Input–output operations	1043
Management information systems	2391	Pretty good privacy	1032
Polish notation	2381	Bell labs relay computers	1013
Syntax, semantics, and pragmatics	1968	Database management system	1001

articles were downloaded at least 1000 times, and not surprisingly, the distribution had a long tail, with 61, or about a tenth of the articles, downloaded fewer than 100 times. Table 7.1 includes the top 40. It is difficult to discern any reason for their being the most popular, as many are not major topics; possibly they were assigned reading in classes.

As to why there was not a 5th edition: After Wiley acquired the ECS, in 2004 it opened discussion about a 5th edition with the three editors. Their idea was for a book of about 1000 pages and 320 articles—by each measure, about half the size of the 4th edition, and more narrowly focused on modern "hot" topics, primarily in new articles, and without the historical content that the editors thought essential to the ECS.[18] Wiley proposed that the fourth-edition editors become senior advisor editors, with others to do the work. They acknowledged that the 4th edition contract said that its editors would receive half the royalties of a subsequent edition if they did no work on it, and said that they had potential new working editors, though it was not clear if those were aware that they'd be working for half-pay. By 2006, Wikipedia had become a significant competitor, and nothing came of the idea. Then in 2020, Hemmendinger heard from a new Wiley editor who wanted to revive the plan for a

---

[18] David Hughes, Wiley editor, email to Ralston, Reilly, Hemmendinger, February 23, 2006.

7.2 ECS Editions, Supplements, and Online Versions

5th edition. They had some exchanges, but after the Wiley editor decided to defer discussion until 2021, it did not resume.

According to an editor of the *Encyclopaedia Britannica*,[19] it is an aphorism that scholars generally regard the previous edition of an encyclopedia as the best one. We believe that the ECS editors would regard the fourth edition as the best, having been quite thoroughly updated. As they disliked what the publisher proposed for a fifth edition, however, this aphorism still applies: at least prospectively, had there been such a fifth edition, the editors would have preferred the fourth.

As we know, Wikipedia began in early 2001, shortly after the 4th edition appeared, and finessed the payment and income-producing problems by being a volunteer enterprise. In its early years, Wikipedia was not always reliable nor well-written. A page on magnetic-core computer memory from the early 2000s, for example, said, "Harvard wasn't interested in the invention, and so Wang sought a patent for it while Woo took ill."[20] According to the Wikipedia documentation of the history of its page on core-memory, a minor variation of the sentence remained until May 8, 2011, after which Woo's health was not mentioned. In recent years, however, Wikipedia articles have been much better written and documented and kept mostly up to date—an impressive achievement for a volunteer activity. Some articles express author biases, but they are generally flagged by volunteer editors, as are articles that are too heavily technical or based on limited or unreliable sources.

---

[19] Ashmore 1962, p. 16.

[20] Centre for Computing History, www.computinghistory.org.uk/sec/3433/Core-Memory, accessed May 5, 2025. The page is extracted from Wikipedia, though the quote is not in the current Wikipedia version but appeared in the June 17, 2005 version.

Chapter 8
Cultural Artifact

Abstract Unlike most of the previous chapters, which have been about the making of an encyclopedia, this chapter is about the cultural meaning of an encyclopedia generally and the Encyclopedia of Computer Science in particular. Topics include, among others, the encyclopedia as an icon of the effort for a person to self-educate or for parents to help educate their children; as a representation of the current state of knowledge of the world around us; or as an indicator that a family or a nation has arrived at a certain station in the world.

8.1 Encyclopedia Scholars on the Encyclopedia as a Cultural Artifact

In addition to its most straightforward use as an information source, an encyclopedia is an artifact with a larger cultural, social, or intellectual meaning that "revolve[s] around materials, places, emotions and personal relations."[1] In this section we point to several of these meanings that have been discussed by encyclopedia scholars, particularly Jutta Haider and Olof Sundin.

As a memory of a material object. They observe that in a survey of readers of *Encyclopaedia Britannica,*

> Many reader comments distinguish… between instrumental use and emotional use, which is typically entwined with memories from the person's past. The encyclopedic sets are talked about in terms of their materiality, a physical presence that many comments refer to. The strong and mostly positive memories conjured up with memories of encyclopedias make it also emotionally difficult for people to physically get rid of the encyclopedias, even in those cases where the owner cannot motivate any practical value for keeping them.[2]

The encyclopedia might be associated in the user's mind, for example, with devouring any copy at hand when they came home from school.

As an instance of the social construction of knowledge. The philosopher Robin McKenna, developing an idea of the philosopher of science Helen Longino,

---

[1] Haider and Sundin 2014, unpaginated (2nd page).

[2] Haider and Sundin 2014, unpaginated (5th page).

has discussed the scientific creation of knowledge, when viewed as a social phenomenon:[3]

> On Longino's picture, the processes that generate justification for scientific hypotheses and theories are social processes. Put roughly, the idea is that a scientific claim or theory is justified when it emerges (relatively) unscathed from critical interactions between scientists.... Longino is interested in the sorts of justificatory reasoning that scientists engage in rather than the logical and evidential relations between theories and the observational data that support them.... Longino's take on the underdetermination problem is to focus on how it is resolved in practice by working scientists. What happens in practice is that background assumptions – substantive and methodological hypotheses, values, prejudices, ideologies, tacit theoretical and metaphysical commitments and views – help fill the gap, but these background assumptions are usually not made explicit. ...The basic picture is that justification – and so knowledge – emerges from social interaction. In these interactions, background assumptions are identified, criticized and defended. The thought is that assumptions that have survived critical scrutiny can be legitimately used to bridge the gap between observation and theory.

In this light, the encyclopedia can then be regarded as an artifact of the scientific creation of knowledge by which a set of authors, reviewers, and editors have engaged in a conversation about what knowledge is worthy of being presented to the public and the way in which it should be presented.

As a token of appreciation for earlier values concerning knowledge and education. As the encyclopedia scholars Haider and Sundin say, the print encyclopedia is an icon of an earlier era when people valued expertise, knowledge, and education. They contrast this with the era of the online encyclopedia, such as Wikipedia:[4]

> Wikipedia is attempting to commoditize knowledge by making it so democratic that it no longer has any flavor—the flavor of a single, unifying intellect. We've already done it with consumer goods, with food, with travel, with college educations, and even with our cities, nearly all of which look as if stamped from the same strip-mall making assembly line.
>
> For many the transition from print to digital seems to go hand in hand with alienation pervasive in capitalist society and also the transition from a perceived stability of modernity (civilization) to the shifting grounds of late modernity and is in this way connected to an increased sense of insecurity ...

As a tool for the autodidact. Haider and Sundin point out that an encyclopedia is a tool for the autodidact to gain mastery of the world. This seems particularly valuable in the field of computing, where so many people who program did not receive a formal education in computer science, but instead learned on the job or taught themselves.

> ...one reader emphasizes that "an encyclopedia is not just to look things up in—it's to gain encyclopedic knowledge of the world!" Here encyclopedias seen as external memory

---

[3] McKenna 2022, p. 2. Menagarishvili 2012 makes a similar point about education rather than science, speaking of dictionaries but equally true of encyclopedias: "As cultural objects, dictionaries perform several types of cultural work. First of all, they have the ability to influence knowledge legitimation as powerful tools for education."

[4] Haider and Sundin 2014.

8.1 Encyclopedia Scholars on the Encyclopedia as a Cultural Artifact 65

resources seem to be perceived as becoming more instrumental and fact-oriented than earlier with their move from print to digital.[5]

As a symbol of social advancement. Haider and Sundin point to the print encyclopedia—here referring in particular to *Britannica*—not as a tool for accessing information but instead as a symbol of knowledge.

> [The encyclopedia] is given a cultural meaning that communicated social advancement to an aspiring middle class: "was it really the books themselves that we all loved, or the fact that we could display them to others and feel smarter because they crowded our shelves?...
>
> There are numerous accounts on how people have used encyclopedias for formal school purposes or for self-initiated learning. Connected to this emerges another role for encyclopedias, namely as a marker of status and as vehicles for cultural and personal identity construction. Here the encyclopedia—as a print artifact—is often a symbol for an aspiring middle class, signaling stability and order or—as a digital service—a symbol for cultural shifts, which are positively or negatively charged."[6]

As a marker of class. The ownership and public display of an encyclopedia is a cultural marker of aspiration or belonging to a particular social class. Haider and Sundin report on the comments of another encyclopedia user:[7]

> I realized my boyfriend's family would mesh with mine, despite being from a different continent, ethnicity and cultural background, when I saw their Encyclopedia on the shelf. I knew they also knew how it ended. Asking them to show me their Google search history or recent Wiki lookups wouldn't go over so well.

As a tool for parents. Buying a set of encyclopedias was regarded as a sacrifice that parents made for their general education: "*Encyclopaedia Britannica* was often bought as a resource for the children to help them achieve in school: 'I was fortunate to have parents who could afford to have a set in our home when I was growing up.'"[8] Parents might similarly buy a computer science encyclopedia for their technically inclined children to encourage their interest in a well-paying occupation.

---

[5] Haider and Sundin 2014, unpaginated (6th page). However, Couch (p. 20) argues that "Encyclopedias can help in the gaining of command of the basic tools of learning, but they cannot take the place of teachers, textbooks, and libraries."
Also, as Sutton 1962 (p. 29) notes, encyclopedias' being identified with an earlier era could have negative impacts—that encyclopedias were identified as "'old fashioned' like gentlemen's libraries or 'monumental buildings shaped like temples'". Sills 1969 (p. 1173) makes a similar point: "A major reason for the general lack of interest in a new encyclopedia was surely the lowered prestige of encyclopedias generally; it seems that a generation ago scholars consulted the *Encyclopedia Britannica* more frequently than they do now, and that for many scholars today an encyclopedia is an expensive set of books containing third-hand material that a salesman tries to persuade them that they must buy if they have the best interests of their children at heart. Moreover, in this age of the computer-generated abstract service, how can an encyclopedia be anything but an outmoded form of publication?"

[6] Haider and Sundin 2014, unpaginated (8th page).

[7] Haider and Sundin 2014, unpaginated (7th page).

[8] Haider and Sundin 2014, unpaginated (7th page). The interior quotation is a quotation from a survey of users of the encyclopedia.

Anthropomorphism of the print encyclopedia. Haider and Sundin note that many users had a close relationship to their print copy of *Encyclopaedia Britannica* and that they felt sadness or loss when it was no longer a regular part of their daily lives. With the announcement of the end of the print version, a user wrote, "'this announcement is like losing an old friend: another victim of the Internet.' ... For many *Encyclopaedia Britannica's* announcement triggered memories of the past and many comments revolved around childhood memories. In families' everyday doings encyclopedias were given meaning."[9]

As a tool of ideology, Western bias, or chronological bias. Menagarishvili writes, "Another cultural issue discussed in current literature is the role played by ideology in dictionaries."[10] This might occur with an encyclopedia by the choice that the editors make to include material about participants who are underrepresented in the domain the encyclopedia addresses. Sills makes a similar point, regarding the social sciences encyclopedia with which he was involved: "The social sciences themselves are products of Western intellectual life, and in that sense the new Encyclopedia will have a distinctive Western bias; the subject matter of the social sciences, however, is international, and we hope that the articles will be intelligible, and meaningful and useful to readers throughout the World."[11] Sills also points out how the dictionary can reflect the bias of a particular period:

> This conceptual model was developed in our staff meetings, in our discussions with the field editors, and in our informal conversations. The "style" and "tone" of the encyclopedia that emerged is partly the result of the reconciliation of our individual points of view; partly as a consequence of the fact that the editorial staff had all been graduate students in the remarkable decade of the 1950's, when the social sciences acquired much of their contemporary empirical-theoretical character, and partly a reflection of the "behavioral sciences" orientation of the field editors."[12]

As a tool to stabilize scientific knowledge and public knowledge. Haider and Sundin note that another scholar, Bernd Frohman, had discussed the epistemological role of an encyclopedia in stabilizing scientific knowledge in the scientific community, and Haider and Sundin argued that a similar role was played by the encyclopedia in stabilizing general knowledge among the public. Frohman differentiated between "an epistemological discourse and a practice discourse of science, where the first relates to the communication of the epistemic content of science and the latter to the stabilizing of science and the scientific system of establishing trustworthiness."[13] The encyclopedia plays the practical role, in essence, of assuring that a particular body of knowledge is regarded as true and representative of the knowledge in a particular domain, such as general science or computer science in particular.[14]

---

[9] Haider and Sundin 2014, unpaginated (5th page).
[10] Menagarishvili 2012.
[11] Sills 1962.
[12] Sills 1969, pp. 1172–1173.
[13] Haider and Sundin 2014, unpaginated (2nd page).
[14] Notwithstanding, Sullivan 1962. (p. 318) cites the argument of Frank Kafker on reservations scholar have about encyclopedias: "Most encyclopedias are multi-volume; they often go into several

As a tool to create value from knowledge. Encyclopedias can be powerful because of their order and accessibility, and the fact that the general reader knows that the encyclopedia is a place to find answers to their problems. Or as the scholar Menagarishvili argues: "The ability to transform knowledge into value has been identified as one of the most important social functions of scientific and technical communication."[15]

To create a postmodern document. Since the late nineteenth century, encyclopedists had not tried to create a master order with the organization of their book. Instead, they had used an alphabetic order, which represented a view of the world as unordered—consistent with a postmodern view of the world and of scholarship.[16]

To attain community support and engage a set of scholars who bought into the organization and content of the encyclopedia. The writing of an encyclopedia can be a powerful organizing activity within a scholarly community. The editors get better known to the authors, and the authors and editors get better known to the readers.[17] The process of selecting the topics to be covered, the editing of the articles, and the selection of links between articles can be a powerful way to reconsider the content of an academic field, as well as to stir new needs and opportunities statements. The result can be a repurposing of the relevant academic communities.[18] The power these encyclopedias hold may be invisible, as Menagarishvili points out in his discussion of dictionaries:

> dictionaries have been dictating what knowledge is valuable and trustworthy (the knowledge found in dictionaries) and what is not (the knowledge omitted by dictionaries). However, because dictionaries are often viewed as mundane documents, their power is invisible, which makes them even stronger.[19]

To promote an objective view of knowledge of the subject matter. Numerous scholars had criticized Peukert's encyclopedia for being subjective and old-fashioned instead of being objective, which had become an important characteristic of all encyclopedias.

---

editions, which may contradict each other; they cover so many disciplines that only a Renaissance man would feel comfortable attempting to comprehend their contents; and, once understood, they are difficult to interpret, because they tend to lack a thesis and even coherence."

Rauch 2005 discusses similar points when he discusses the encyclopedia as a "public service" and as a "scientific endeavor".

[15] Menagarishvili 2012.

[16] Fenske 2010. It is also interesting to see Rajan, who discusses French and Scottish encyclopedias of the eighteenth and nineteenth centuries as *positivist*.

[17] However, there is also a sense of community even when the members do not meet, as Menagarishvili 2012 (p. 3) observes, using the term "imagined communities" that had been coined by Benedict Anderson, "that can be defined as communities consisting of people who 'will never know most of their fellow-members, meet them, or even hear of them, yet in the minds of each lives the image of their communion'" (see Anderson 2006).

[18] Fenske 2010. Sutton 1962 (pp. 28–29) discusses how the idea for a. social sciences encyclopedia got both the Social Sciences Research Council and the Ford Foundation engaged in the planning for an encyclopedia, as well as dozens of individual scholars as consultants and reviewers. Sills 1962 (p. 32) discusses how ten social science disciplines supported the new social science encyclopedia.

[19] Menagarishvili 2012, p. 1.

Peuckert's critics preferred an "objective" manner of working, without considering that objectivity itself is a construction. Among other things, *objectivity* implied neutrality, detachment, and standardized practices of knowledge production and representation that could be delivered only by experts [as opposed to being incomplete, subjective, and unsystematic]. Objective instruments like type-indexes and a neutral style of reasoning were preferred.[20]

As a sign of rebuilding culture after the ravages of economic depression and war. There was an enthusiasm for education following the Great Depression and the Second World War, as witnessed by the large number of GIs who enrolled in college, often at government expense. It was seen as a way to get on with life and build a way forward for individuals, their families, and society as a whole. There was a boom in encyclopedia projects after the war, which fits well with this mentality.[21]

As an expression of nationalism. An encyclopedia can be crowning achievement, or as the historian of technology Lynn Thorndike said, "the most important monuments of the history of science and civilisation."[22] For Germany in particular, with its losses in the two world wars in the twentieth century, their encyclopedia projects were a way of reestablishing its earlier leadership in the academic disciplines. As Sullivan noted, "the appearance of new encyclopedias were also symptoms of the spirit of independent nationalism in budding republics. Encyclopedia projects were patronized by the new national governments and directed by the national academies of arts and sciences."[23]

8.2 ECS as a Cultural Object

Encyclopedias are not all created equal. Some, the *Encyclopaedia Britannica* in particular, are cultural artifacts of great weight. They represent knowledge accumulated over several centuries and presented to readers in authoritative accounts. Multivolume encyclopedias stand out in their physical bulk—material representations of knowledge and culture—and by virtue of their authority. They are guides for the perplexed and tools for the education of youth, often bought by parents who hope to raise their children well—or simply to raise their seating with a thick volume. As they may belong to families for decades, they have sentimental value that makes them hard to give up.

How does the one-volume *Encyclopedia of Computer Science* fare? It is scarcely 50 years old and devoted to a subject that continues to change in its foundations, in its applications and societal impact, and in the educational strategies through which it is taught. The book does have ample bulk for a single volume, more suited to a desktop

---

[20] Fenske 2010, p. 67. She points to Daston and Galison 2007 in discussion of this point.

[21] France 1998.

[22] Sullivan 1990, p. 315.

[23] Sullivan 1990, p. 332; a similar point is made by Fenske 2010, about the use of the folklore encyclopedia by German folklore scholars to regain their leading position in the international folklore community.

8.2 ECS as a Cultural Object

than to being held in the hand or lap; Wiley's 2008 reprint of the ECS was in two volumes. A review that praised the book said that it covered the field superficially, not in depth,[24] consistent with Ralston's first-edition foreword that described the ECS as comprehensive in *breadth* though not in *depth*, being intended for the nonspecialist.[25]

As we commented in Chap. 2, the information that we do have about the ECS use is largely indirect. Perhaps due both to its size and its subject, far narrower than an entire culture, the ECS did not appear to generate strong emotions of attachment or otherwise; at least the editors did not hear of them. That contrasts with the attachment that readers (or owners) of major encyclopedias reported, who may have held a volume in their lap as their dog rested at their feet (the wife of one author did once have her dog in her lap as the ECS sat at her feet).

One account of the growth in the number of encyclopedias is that it was "a reaction to the mental and physical destruction of World War II"[26]. As the ECS project began more than a quarter century later, it was not such a direct reaction. The military origin of digital computing has been well-documented,[27] however, having started during that war and continued during the Cold War that followed. The ECS addresses what emerged from that origin, but it pays rather little attention to wartime developments themselves. The term "Second World War" is not in the index of any of the editions, nor does the ECS discuss table-making either as the work of human computers or of automatic ones. "Ballistics" is mentioned in passing in an article on early digital computers, which says that ENIAC was intended for ballistics calculations, though it became more general. There is a long article on analog computing in the first three ECS editions, which mentions a gun-director computer briefly but is largely about the design of analog computers in general. A much shorter article in the fourth edition has a brief paragraph on mechanical analog gunnery computers. Its article on the differential analyzer used to solve differential equations such as those for gunnery tables does not mention ballistics, and the ENIAC article also says only briefly that it was intended to replace the slower mechanical differential analyzer at the US Army Ballistics Research Laboratory. The US Advanced Research Projects Agency (ARPA) is not in the first-edition index, but has several entries in the fourth edition, each a brief mention of its support for research projects, including Arpanet. In general, though, by the time that the ECS appeared, digital computing had a presence largely separated from its military origins.

As an instance of the social construction of knowledge: If scientific or other knowledge is socially constructed through critical interactions among scientists, then the ECS, like other encyclopedias that embody the state of knowledge of a subject, is also a social construct. Particularly for a subject that is still in the process of being defined, this is a plausible claim; the computer science topics that the ECS addresses are those whose importance or utility has been established by agreement among authors and other specialists. The articles on formal grammars and languages, for

---

[24] Landis 1976, p. 12.

[25] Ralston 1976, p. viii.

[26] Fenske, p 52

[27] Edwards 1997; Akera 2007.

example, are there because there is common agreement that they are an appropriate way to analyze computations. Articles on software engineering are similar, except that the discourse about its foundations and methods is much more in flux and with far less agreement; it is a subject still in the making.

An encyclopedia preface may manifest its editors' intent. The preface of the first edition of the ECS is quite brief, stating Ralston's view that the discipline is ready for a snapshot of its state, one that has both breadth and depth, and that its useful life will be a half-decade or more—much longer for some of it. In the next edition, seven years later, the editors wrote, "The first edition of an encyclopedia is one of those tasks which must be undertaken so that it may be done right the next time."[28] Doing it right included having 90 new articles, and 140 rewritten ones most extensively, resulting in 40% new material The prefaces of the following two editions continued the theme; getting it right meant more revisions and additions, as well as new useful appendices. All the prefaces asked readers for corrections and suggestions of new material; we do not know how often the latter were made. The fourth-edition preface added that the editors intended to make the book available by subscription on the World Wide Web and hoped to keep it up to date as a print edition could not be. They anticipated that eventually, although not for a fifth edition, the ECS would be entirely online. As we have seen, none of that came to pass, and the online encyclopedia is not the ECS.

Some reflections on the ECS as a cultural artifact: For some decades, the computing profession and computer science more narrowly has been predominately male. One account[29] is that while women had initially had a large presence, once the field became a profession, men took over. This view has been disputed,[30] but today and for some years, women have been in the minority. The ECS is no exception; 5% of the first-edition authors were women, and the percentage rose to 10 or 11% for the third and fourth, well below the 20–25% of women computer scientists today. Although the percentage of women receiving undergraduate computer science degrees in the mid-1980s rose to 35% before declining to its current level, the percentage of women who would have established their credentials and be likely to become ECS authors would have been much smaller in the early 1970s and even in the mid-1990s. The ECS authorship was thus consistent with the state of the field, but the ECS was far from being a leader in contributing to an appropriate status for women.

The third edition was the first to have an article on Women in Computing, a scant two pages, which increased to three pages in the fourth edition. The first version began, "Despite the success of women such as the late Rear Admiral Grace Murray Hopper (q.v.), women are severely underrepresented...." The next version began more positively, "Women have played a primary role in computer programming since its origins in the mid-1800s," and went on to point out their early roles. Both articles tabulated the fractions of women in degree programs and discussed reasons for those

---

[28] Ralston & Reilly 1983, p. xi.
[29] Ensmenger 2012.
[30] Misa 2024.

8.2 ECS as a Cultural Object   71

numbers not being higher. The fourth edition listed notable women in the field and described institutional efforts to increase their numbers. Given their length, neither article went deeply into the reasons for there being too few women in the field, although they mentioned issues such as the male hacker culture as a discouragement.

Technological convergence has become a popular topic, and one of its early instances is the convergence of communication and computing in cell phones, email and texting, and at a lower level, in the digital switches that route telephone traffic. The ECS has had a Communication and Computers article from the start, and it is interesting to see its evolution. The first-edition article was almost entirely about network message switching (which should have been called packet switching) such as the Arpanet used. It briefly mentions the switches used in telephony, which had been electromechanical but had recently become digital. The second-edition article, by a new author, continued the attention to digital switching systems for networking and telephony, but added sections on legal and on political issues. The former addressed the regulation of hybrid data processing and communication services and possible revisions of the 1934 Communications Act. The latter was about the problems of information flow between countries. It also mentioned the growing use of personal computers that could draw on databases and use the developing "personal computer networks"—a quite new possibility in 1982.

The third-edition article expanded parts of the preceding one but did not change its focus; and despite its being a decade later, did not change its brief discussion of personal-computing networking, a subject that Rankin has described well.[31] The fourth-edition article was written by Marjory Blumenthal, head of the Computer Science and Telecommunications Board of the US National Research Council. The article, which starts, "*Computing* is increasingly inseparable from *communications*," does not address implementation details, which had been covered in networking articles even in the first edition. Instead, it focused on trends in networking, computing in mass markets, and public policy. These changes in the article were a good example of the ECS keeping up with social and policy issues as well as technical ones.

The theme of a recent book on computing history is that computing is now many things.[32] Some have been there since the early days of digital computing: the computer as a scientific tool, a data processing tool, a control system, and an interactive tool. Others are more recent: a communications platform, office equipment, a graphical tool, a universal media device, a publishing platform, and a network. These multiple roles of computing would be familiar to the ECS reader, as all its editions have had articles on these topics, although of course the more recent ones were not addressed in the early editions. Some of these topics had not become central even at the time of the fourth edition, as its articles are now 25 to 30 years old in 2025. Commercial cellular networks for telephony appeared only in the early 1990s, remote computers (the cloud) for networked storage were just developing, and the IEEE 802.11 standard for wireless networking dates to 1997. The article on desktop publishing was current in the late 1990s but much more could be said on the topic

---

[31] Rankin 2018.
[32] Haigh & Ceruzzi 2021.

now. In short, the ECS was up to date when it appeared, but a new edition now would have to give much more attention to the multiple roles of computing, though it would be difficult not to continue to have the articles on technical fundamentals.

As a tool for the autodidact; It would be a mistake to regard the ECS as an explicit effort to resist what Haider and Sundin[33] calls the move to "commoditize knowledge" by making it flavorless. Nevertheless, with the publication of the 4th edition in 2000, coinciding with the appearance of Wikipedia, it is an account of computer science and computing more generally that is told by experts and that offers an education in the subject, eminently suitable as a starting point for an autodidact.

---

[33] Haider and Sundin 2014, quoting the *New York Times*.

Chapter 9
An Intellectual Field and Its Reference Tools

Abstract This chapter discusses the changing landscape for encyclopedias of computing, the reasons why the *Encyclopedia of Computer Science* flourished in the last quarter of the twentieth century, competitors to this encyclopedia, and ways in which this study might be extended.

There was a limited window of time for the *Encyclopedia of Computer Science*—the leading encyclopedia covering the field of computing—to be created and flourish, roughly coeval with the last quarter of the twentieth century. This window of opportunity for creating and marketing computing reference tools in print form rapidly closed—or at least became much less economically feasible—with the opportunity to create electronic versions that could be distributed in CD or DVD format and on the Internet.

Books on digital computation for a general audience are nearly as old as modern stored-program digital computers.[1] A 1971 exhibit at the IBM Exhibit Center in New York City told the story of digital computation starting with Herman Hollerith's tabulating machines used in the 1890 US census (with a brief look back to Charles Babbage).[2] The *Encyclopedia of Computer Science*, however, was the first comprehensive presentation of the entire field of computing, intended for a general audience but with sufficient detail to meet the needs of computing professionals as well. It is surely unusual for a 1500-page encyclopedia to be edited by one person with no editorial staff except for one assistant, and the success of the ECS depended heavily on Anthony Ralston's organizational skills that led him to become president of the Association for Computing Machinery and on his wide acquaintance with leaders in the many areas of computer science that was a result of that role.

By 1976, computing had become an established technical field and had a significant role in business and industry. University computer science departments were being established, and computers had just begun to enter households. The ECS addressed all these aspects of computing: it was many things to many people. Its

---

[1] See, for example, Berkeley 1949.
[2] Eames and Eames 1973.

articles on technical topics were accessible to college students and useful for professionals. Those on computing in other fields provided an up-to-date account of the many applications of computing, and articles on computing history and its societal aspects were generally accessible accounts of those areas. All of these expanded in subsequent editions.

A look at the data shows a strong correlation between the editions of ECS and college undergraduate computer science degrees. The ECS editions appeared every seven years (except for the third edition, which was delayed by editor illness). In the interval between the first two editions, enrollment increased 400%! It continued to grow after 1983, when the second edition appeared, but when the third failed to appear in 1990, enrollment began to decline, reversed only three years later with publication of the third edition. We can only speculate as to whether causation, not only correlation, was at play here.

One issue for an encyclopedia devoted to a rapidly changing subject is its timeliness. Unlike some more general encyclopedias, the ECS did not publish a yearbook to cover current events. It did succeed in being generally up to date to the extent permitted by the typical seven-year interval between editions, particularly if we keep in mind that work on an edition began several years before its publication. In computer networking, for example, the Arpanet, started in 1969, had an entry in the 1976 edition. At that time, research on the TCP/IP protocol used in the current Internet, had begun, though it did not see widespread use before the Arpanet adopted it at the start of 1983. The second ECS edition articles were written by the start of the 1980s, at which time TCP/IP was still a research project, and it is only in retrospect that we can know that it was a success. Similarly, the 1993 third ECS edition discusses TCP/IP but contains no article about it, although it has an article about the Open Systems Interconnection (OSI) protocols, which at the time appeared likely to become a standard; however, eventually they were superseded by TCP/IP, a related approach.

As another example, "personal computing" was a term used in popular magazines as early as 1975, following the 1974 production of the Altair hobbyist computing kit—too late for the first ECS edition. The second edition, however, did include a five-page article on the topic, which discussed the early personal computers such as the Radio Shack TRS/80, the Commodore Pet, and the Apple II, and was sufficiently current to refer to the state of activity in 1982 and the recent appearance of the IBM PC. The next two editions kept up with the topic.

The production of the ECS remained a very lean operation through its four editions. Fundraising was never necessary; the publishers funded its production with payments to editorial boards, reviewers, and at times, an assistant. Ralston was joined by first one and then two co-editors, and while the first three editions had editorial boards, they were largely advisory. The editors recruited the authors and did all the editing, with some record-keeping help from a part-time assistant and from the publishers. The success of the ECS was due in large part to the quality of its authors, 20 of whom are among the 81 recipients of the Turing Award, the major award in computer science; that includes eight of the 11 recipients in the first decade of the award. Many of the other authors were recognized at the time or later with other major computing awards. At the risk of immodesty, as one of us co-edited the fourth edition, we believe that the breadth of the editors' knowledge also contributed to this strength.

As we remarked earlier, editors do not generally know who reads their encyclopedias. We do know that even 25 years after its publication, when some of its articles are inevitably dated, the fourth ECS edition remains on college library reference shelves. Its articles in the ACM Digital Library continue to be read. Authors' Web sites often list their ECS articles among their publications. Reviews in professional publications and in library journals describe the ECS as the standard reference in its field. Thus, for the quarter century of the ECS editions and for the following quarter century, the volume has remained the most significant encyclopedia of computing for a wide range of readers.[3]

ECS was not the only encyclopedia of computer science, as we showed in a table in Chap. 1. While there are several other one- or two-volume encyclopedias of computing, none rival the ECS in scope, appropriate level, and authoritativeness. We will mention just three of these competing works here. The *Encyclopedia of Computer Science and Technology,* edited by Harry Henderson,[4] is part of the Facts on File Science Library and is written at a relatively low level, intended for secondary schools. Its articles are largely a page or less in length, with 600 articles in 525 pages. It has short explanations of common terms such as "webcam", "phishing", and "cascading style sheet". Its articles on more technical subjects elide detail; the article on concurrent programing, for example, does not explain what an atomic operation is—a fundamental concept. The article on programming languages is the same length as one on programming as a profession—a page each. This reference work thus serves better as a collection of brief explanations than as an encyclopedia.

The *Encyclopedia of Computer Science and Technology,* edited by Phillip Laplante,[5] apparently serves the same audience as ECS but its nature is quite different. It has 88 articles in 885 pages[6] and so they average 10 pages rather than the one page typical in Henderson's encyclopedia. It lists 126 authors, although the editor's preface says that some articles were not newly created but instead gleaned from its publisher's other books. According to the preface, LaPlante's encyclopedia is intended for technology professionals, as well as information science students. Its articles are written as independent chapters; they do not show the significant editorial work of ECS in connecting topics and articles with one another. Many of these articles use mathematical notation familiar to computer science students and professionals, although perhaps not to all readers. There are no cross-references among articles, though notation used without explanation in one article may be explained in another, as the

---

[3] The 2010 final print edition of the *Britannica* sold 12,000 copies [https://www.theguardian.com/books/2012/apr/05/encyclopedia-britannica-final-print-edition], only slightly more than sales of each of the first three editions, and far less than second-edition sales through a book club. It is difficult to compare sales of the best-known multivolume encyclopedia with a single volume like the ECS.

[4] Henderson 2009.

[5] Laplante 2017.

[6] The book's Web site says 1500 articles, perhaps referring to an extended online version.

"big-Oh" notation is used in the "Classes: NP and NP-Complete" article but defined only in the "Algorithms" one. The selection of topics is unusual; for example, the first 11 articles (80 pages, or 9% of the book) are on 3-D graphics. There is an article on (formal) languages, one on domain-specific ("little") programming languages, and one on programming languages for concurrency, but none programming languages in general. The "LDPC Decoders: Acceleration" article is about parallel programming with graphics processing units but never mentions or defines its title topic.[7]

The *Encyclopedia of Computers and Computer History*, edited by Raúl Rojas[8], has 600 articles, about the same number as in the ECS, but in 930 pages, less than half the ECS length. It has about a third as many authors as does the ECS, with many of the articles written by the editor or his staff. One review comments that some articles reproduce earlier errors and depend on autobiographical accounts.[9] This encyclopedia focuses more on the technology than on computer uses, although it is the only one of these encyclopedias with "history" in its title.

Chapter 7 described some reasons for there not being a fifth ECS edition, including the growth of online reference works. There may be a more fundamental reason for its having ended with the fourth edition in 2000. That chapter also discussed changes in several articles through the four editions and over a quarter century, observing that as the field matured, there needed to be less attention to technical details in understanding the uses of computing. Those details are still important for specialists, but unlike the earlier days of computing, one can use computer programs without attending to them; just as books on automobile transportation can be about social, political, and legal issues rather than about how internal combustion engines or electric motors work. There is still a need for works on such internal details, but as computers become more complex, these details are increasingly intended for specialists—so these are more like handbooks than encyclopedias. The level of detail in the most recent ECS edition may well be as far as one can go with a reference work for a general audience. Books that present the subject for a wide audience now are more likely to have titles such as "What is …?", akin to Courant and Robbins' classic book *What is Mathematics?*[10] One of the best of this genre on computer science is David Harel's *Algorithmics: The Spirit of Computing*.[11] In short, the ECS has had an important role, but now has done its job.

There would have been no incentive to create ECS until there was an established body of information about computers and until the computer had proved itself to have societal import. Thus, the appearance of this encyclopedia, together with other specialized reference tools—such as handbooks, dictionaries, and chronologies about

---

[7] There are also omissions and errors; the article on concurrency mentions semaphores and monitors without explanation, and those terms are not in the index. The "Classes" article says that the NP class consists of problems that almost certainly do not have polynomial-time solutions, although later it correctly says that as the class P of problems with polynomial-time solutions is contained in NP, some NP problems have efficient solutions.

[8] Rojas 2001.

[9] Akera 2004.

[10] Courant and Robbins 1996.

[11] Harel 2004.

computing—marked the maturation of computing in Western society. This suggests a new approach to studying the emergence of computing as an academic discipline and a viable activity in Western society—by seeing how the new reference artifacts emerged and changed over time. We leave this task to future scholarship.

The encyclopedia is a complex information tool, at least to create if not to use. It involves the investment of time of at least hundreds of busy professional individuals and the near total devotion of a few senior editors. Anthony Ralston has published a first-hand account of how this encyclopedia came about, and the challenges of creating and distributing the four editions. We welcome Ralston's personal observations, but we believe there is more to say in light of the experience of other encyclopedia projects. There is a sizable literature about the history and nature of reference tools, and we have drawn on that literature to provide an academic account of the creation of the *Encyclopedia of Computer Science*. This account has shown the complexity of identifying an audience, creating a stance and style, establishing content guidelines, establishing and enacting a complex editorial process, procuring funding for the process, and finding a publisher and working with them to create and market the encyclopedia. We have discussed issues related to subsequent editions and online versions. Finally, we have discussed this encyclopedia and encyclopedias in general as a cultural artifact, which may have many different cultural meanings, only some of which were envisioned by the editors of the encyclopedia.

Most of the editors and advisory board members of the *Encyclopedia of Computer Science* are no longer alive to ask about how this encyclopedia came about. So, instead, we consulted this rich literature on encyclopedia history to identify key issues about the creation and place in society of both general-purpose and specialized encyclopedias (the first sections in Chapters Two through Eight); and then we used these insights to try to gain a better understanding of the *Encyclopedia of Computer Science* (the second sections in Chapters Two through Eight). In several instances, we identified issues that we as historians of encyclopedias would like to know about, even though we could not always answer them about our specific encyclopedia in question.

We believe that scholars interested in studying encyclopedias and other reference tools, their place as markers of the establishment of a mature academic discipline, and their multiple roles as cultural artifacts can learn from our general discussion of encyclopedias in the first section of each chapter of this study. Thus, we have included in those sections of this work some questions that we believe are valuable to the study of an encyclopedia, even when we have not been able to provide specific answers about ECS. Thus, one might argue that these sections provide a template for the future study of encyclopedias. We have discussed both general encyclopedias (e.g., *Funk & Wagnalls, Britannica*) and various specialized encyclopedias covering such fields as folklore, music, and the social sciences. Our template in the initial sections can be used to analyze general encyclopedias, but it is even more valuable in the analysis of specialized encyclopedias. The second sections of each chapter give a detailed account of the experiences in creating yet another successful encyclopedia—one from yet another discipline (computing). Thus, in addition to providing specific information about ECS that might be useful to computer historians, they also provide another example of an analyzed special encyclopedia that might be valuable to any scholar interested in analyzing a special encyclopedia, no matter what domain of knowledge it covers.

There are some obvious ways to extend this study. One can conduct detailed comparisons of this encyclopedia with other print and electronic encyclopedias about computing. One could examine the affordances of online presentation and determine how they enhance or detract from user experience with these encyclopedias. One could examine some of the other reference tools for computing, such as handbooks and dictionaries, see how they inform the study of the maturation of computing, or provide a snapshot of what was known and how people thought about computing at a particular point in time. All of these would be additions to the intellectual and cultural history of computing as it is presently practiced.

Bibliography

Akera, A. 2004. Review of Rojas, *Encyclopedia of Computers and Computer History*. *IEEE Annals of the History of Computing* 26 (2): 90.
Akera, A. 2007. *Calculating a Natural World*. Cambridge, MA: MIT Press.
Anderson, B. 2006. *Imagined Communities: Reflections on the Origin and Spread of Nationalism*. New York, NY: Verso.
Ashmore, H.S. 1962. Editing the Universal Encyclopedia. *The American Behavioral Scientist* 6 (1): 15–18.
Aspray, W. (ed.). 2024. *Writing Computer and Information History*. Rowman & Littlefield.
Auchter, D. 1999. The Evolution of the *Encyclopaedia Britannica*: From the Macropaedia to Britannica Online. *Reference Services Review* 27 (3): 291–299.
Barzun, J. 1962. Notes on the Making of a World Encyclopedia. *The American Behavioral Scientist* 6 (1): 7–14.
Bates, M.J. 2007. Defining the Information Disciplines in Encyclopedia Development. *Information Research* 12 (4). https://informationr.net/ir/12-4/colis/colis29.html. Accessed July 2, 2025.
Bates, M.J. 2025. An Operational Definition of the Information Disciplines. *University of Illinois Graduate School of Library and Information Science, 2010.* http://pages.gseis.ucla.edu/faculty/bates/articles/pdf/Contribution512-1.pdf. Accessed July 2, 2025.
Bates, M.J., and M.N. Maack. 2009. *Encyclopedia of Library and Information Sciences*, 3rd ed. Boca Raton, FL: CRC Press.
Berkeley, E.C. 1949. *Giant Brains*. New York: John Wiley & Sons.
Chamberlain, R. 2023. *From Diderot to Software Bot: The Evolution of Encyclopedias in Historical Study* (Doctoral dissertation, Case Western Reserve University).
Couch, W.T. 1962. Encyclopedias and Education. *The American Behavioral Scientist* 6 (1): 19–22.
Courant, R., and H. Robbins. 1996. *What Is Mathematics?* 2nd ed. Oxford University Press.
Danowitz, E.S. 2017. Britannica on the Eve of its 250th Birthday: An Encyclopedia's Metamorphosis. *Reference Reviews* 31 (6): 1–6.
Daston, L., and P. Galison. 2007. *Objectivity*. Princeton University Press.
de Grazia, 1962. A Theory of Encyclopedism. *The American Behavioral Scientist* 6 (1): 38–40.
Denning, P., D.E. Comer, D. Gries, M.C. Mulder, A.B. Tucker, J.A. Turner, and P.R. Young. 1989. Computing as a Discipline. *Communications of the ACM* 32 (1): 9–23.
Diderot, D., and J. le Rond d'Alembert (eds.). 1751–1772. *Encyclopédie*. André Le Breton, Paris, France.
Donato, C. 1993. Eighteenth-Century Encyclopedias and National Identity. *History of European Ideas* 16 (4–6): 959–965.

Downey, G. 2024. Writing Geography into the History of Computing and Information. In *Writing Computer and Information History*, ed. William Aspray, 393–426. Rowman & Littlefield.

Durbin, P.T. 1996. Encyclopedias and the Integration of Knowledge. *Social Epistemology* 10 (1): 123–133.

Eames, C., and R. Eames. 1973. *A Computer Perspective*. Cambridge, MA: Harvard University Press.

Edwards, P.N. 1997. *The Closed World: Computers and the Politics of Discourse in Cold War America*. Cambridge, MA: MIT Press.

Eliade, M. 1973. Dictionaries and Encyclopedias. *History of Religions* 12 (3): 284–295.

Ensmenger, N. 2012. *The Computer Boys Take Over*. Cambridge, MA: MIT Press.

Fenske, M. 2010. The Undoing of an Encyclopedia: Knowledge Practices Within German Folklore Studies After World War II. *Journal of Folklore Research* 47 (1/2): 51–78.

Flanagin, Andrew J., and Miriam J. Metzger. 2011. From *Encyclopaedia Britannica* to Wikipedia: Generational Differences in the Perceived Credibility of Online Encyclopedia Information. *Information, Communication & Society* 14 (3): 355–374.

Forster, E.M. 1909. *The Machine Stops. The Oxford and Cambridge Reviews*. Archibald Constable, UK.

France, P. 1998. The Encyclopedia as Organism. *The European Legacy* 3 (3): 62–75.

Geiger, R.L., and C.K. Anderson. 2017. Review Essay: Encyclopedias as Institutional History. In *History of Higher Education Annual: 2003–2004*, 157–165. Routledge.

Granholm, J.W. 1976. From Access Methods to Konrad Zuse. *Datamation* 22 (11): 122–123.

Greenstein, S. 2012. The Range of Linus' Law. *IEEE Micro* 32 (1): 72.

Greenstein, S. 2017. The Reference Wars: Encyclopædia Britannica's Decline and Encarta's Emergence. *Strategic Management Journal* 38 (5): 995–1017.

Greenstein, S. 2019. An Archetype for Outsiders in Technology Commercialization. In *Historical Studies in Computing, Information, and Society: Insights from the Flatiron Lectures*, ed. William Aspray, 137–172. Cham: Springer International Publishers.

Greenstein, S. 2024. Archetypes of Product Launch by Insiders, Outsiders, and Visionaries. *Industrial and Corporate Change* 33 (1): 216–237.

Greenstein, S., and M. Devereux. 2017a. The Crisis at *Encyclopædia Britannica*. *Kellogg School of Management Cases*, pp. 1–18.

Greenstein, S., and M. Devereux. 2017b. Wikipedia in the Spotlight. *Kellogg School of Management Cases*, pp. 1–18.

Greenstein, S., R. Frazzano, and E. Meagher. 2017. Triumph of the Commons: Wikia and the Commercialization of Open-Source Communities in 2009. *Kellogg School of Management Cases*, pp. 1–24.

Greenstein, S., G. Gu, and F. Zhu. 2021. Ideology and Composition Among an Online Crowd: Evidence from Wikipedians. *Management Science* 67 (5): 3067–3086.

Greenstein, S., and F. Zhu. 2012a. *Collective Intelligence and Neutral Point of View: The Case of Wikipedia* (No. w18167). National Bureau of Economic Research.

Greenstein, S., and F. Zhu. 2012b. Is Wikipedia Biased? *American Economic Review* 102 (3): 343–348.

Greenstein, S., and F. Zhu. 2014. *Do Experts or Collective Intelligence Write with More Bias? Evidence from Encyclopædia Britannica and Wikipedia*. Harvard Business School.

Greenstein, S., and F. Zhu. 2016. Open Content, Linus' Law, and Neutral Point of View. *Information Systems Research* 27 (3): 618–635.

Greenstein, S., and F. Zhu. 2018. Do Experts or Crowd-Based Models Produce More Bias? Evidence from Encyclopedia Britannica and Wikipedia. *MIS Quarterly* 42 (3): 945–960.

Gronas, M., A. Rumshisky, A. Gabrovski, S. Kovaka, and H. Chen. 2012. Tracking the History of Knowledge Using Historical Editions of *Encyclopaedia Britannica*. In *Adaptation of Language Resources and Tools for Processing Cultural Heritage Objects*.

Bibliography

Haider, J., and O. Sundin. 2014. The Materiality of Encyclopedic Information: Remediating a Loved One—Mourning *Britannica*. *Proceedings of the American Society for Information Science and Technology* 51 (1): 1–10.

Haigh, T., and P.E. Ceruzzi. 2021. *A New History of Modern Computing*. Cambridge, MA: MIT Press.

Hancher, M. 2019. Dictionary versus Encyclopedia, Then and Now. *Dictionaries: Journal of the Dictionary Society of North America* 40 (1): 113–138.

Harel, D. 2004. *Algorithmics: The Spirit of Computing*, 3rd ed. Addison-Wesley.

Henderson, H. (ed.). 2009. *Encyclopedia of Computer Science and Technology*. Facts on File Library.

Holman Rector, L. 2008. Comparison of Wikipedia and Other Encyclopedias for Accuracy, Breadth, and Depth in Historical Articles. *Reference Services Review* 36 (1): 7–22.

Kallman, H. 1994. The Making of a One-Country Music Encyclopedia: An Essay after an Encyclopedia. *Fontes Artis Musicae* 41(1): 3–19.

Kitchin, R., and M. Dodge. 2002. *The Atlas of Cyberspace*. Addison-Wesley, Boston, MA. Also at https://kitchin.org/atlas/. Accessed July 3, 2025.

Kruse, P. 1958. *The Story of Encyclopaedia Britannica, 1768–1943* (Doctoral dissertation, The University of Chicago).

Landis, C.P. 1976. Review of *Encyclopedia of Computer Science* by Anthony Ralston, and C.L. Meek (eds.). Petrocelli/Charter.: and *Encyclopedia of Computer Science and Technology* by Jack Belzer, Albert G. Holzman, and Allen Kent, (eds.). Marcel Dekker, Inc.. *Computers and Society,* 7 (Winter, 4): 12.

Laplante, P. (ed.). 2017. *Encyclopedia of Computer Science and Technology*, 2nd ed. CRC Press (Taylor & Francis Group).

Loveland, J. 2019. *The European Encyclopedia: From 1650 to the Twenty-first Century*. Cambridge University Press.

Loveland, J., and J. Reagle. 2019. Wikipedia and Encyclopedic Production. *New Media & Society* 15 (8): 1294–1311.

McKenna, R. 2022. Is Knowledge a Social Phenomenon? *Inquiry*, pp. 1–25.

Menagarishvili, O. 2012. *Dictionaries of Science as Participants in the Scientific Knowledge Economy* (Doctoral dissertation, University of Minnesota).

Messner, M., and M.W. DiStaso. 2013. Wikipedia Versus *Encyclopaedia Britannica*: A Longitudinal Analysis to Identify the Impact of Social Media on the Standards of Knowledge. *Mass Communication and Society* 16 (4): 465–486.

Misa, T.J. 2024. Dynamics of Gender Bias Within Computer Science. *Infomation & Culture* 59 (2): 161–181.

O'Sullivan, D. 2011. What Is an Encyclopedia. In *"From Pliny to Wikipedia." Critical Point of View: A Wikipedia Reader*, ed. Greet Lovink, and Nathaniel Tkacz. Amsterdam: Institute of Network Cultures.

O'Sullivan, J. 2018. How We Made the Wireless Network. *Nature Electronics* 1 (2): 147. https://doi.org/10.1038/s41928-018-0027-y

Pang, Alex Soojung-Kim. 1998. The Work of the Encyclopedia in the Age of Electronic Reproduction. First Monday 3 (9). https://doi.org/10.5210/fm.v3i9.615

Rajan, T. 2007. The Encyclopedia and the Universality of Theory: Idealism and the Organization of Knowledge. *Textual Practice* 21 (2): 335–358.

Ralston, A. 1965. *A First Course in Numerical Analysis*. McGraw-Hill.

Ralston, A. (ed.). 1976. *Encyclopedia of Computer Science*. New York, NY: Petrocelli/Charter.

Ralston, A. 2004. Four Editions and Eight Publishers: A History of the *Encyclopedia of Computer Science*. *IEEE Annals of the History of Computing* 26 (1): 42–52.

Ralston, A., and E.D. Reilly Jr. (eds.). 1983. *Encyclopedia of Computer Science and Engineering*, 2nd ed. New York, NY: Van Nostrand Reinold.

Ralston, A., and E.D. Reilly Jr. (eds.). 1993. *Encyclopedia of Computer Science*, 3rd ed. New York, NY: Van Nostrand Reinold.

Ralston, A., E.D. Reilly Jr., and D. Hemmendinger (eds.). 2000. *Encyclopedia of Computer Science*, 4th ed. New York, NY: Grove Dictionaries (Nature Publishing Group).

Ralston, A., and H.S. Wilf. 1962. *Mathematical Methods for Digital Computing*, John Wiley & Sons.

Randell, D.M. (ed.). 2003. *The Harvard Dictionary of Music*, 4th ed. Cambridge, MA: Harvard University Press.

Rankin, J.L. 2018. *A People's History of Computing in the United States*. Cambridge, MA: Harvard University Press.

Rauch, A. 2005. Review of Richard Yeo. *Encyclopaedic Visions: Scientific Dictionaries and Enlightenment Culture. Isis* 96 (3): 442–443.

Reilly, E.D. Jr. (ed.). 2004. *Concise Encyclopedia of Computer Science*. Chichester, UK: John Wiley & Sons.

Rojas, R. (ed.). 2001. *Encyclopedia of Computers and Computer History*. Fitzroy Dearborn.

Roncaglia, Gino. 2021. Encyclopedias and Encyclopedism in the Era of the Web. *JLIS: Italian Journal of Library, Archives and Information Science, Rivista italiana di biblioteconomia, archivistica e scienza dell'informazione* 12 (3): 69–90.

Rosenzweig, R. 2006. Can History Be Open Source? Wikipedia and the Future of the Past. *The Journal of American History* 93 (1): 117–146.

Rossney, R. 1995. Encyclopaedia Britannica Online? *Wired* 3 (8).

Sills, D.L. 1962. The New *Encyclopedia of the Social Sciences. The American Behavioral Scientist* 6 (1): 31–34.

Sills, D.L. 1969. Editing a Scientific Encyclopedia. *Science* 163 (3872): 1169–1175.

Stecchini, L.C. 1962. On Encyclopedias in Time and Space. *The American Behavioral Scientist* 6 (1): 3–5.

Stover, C.F. 1962. Change and Rationality in Encyclopedism. *The American Behavioral Scientist* 6 (1): 35–38.

Stvilia, B., M.B. Twidale, L.C. Smith, and L. Gasser. 2005. Assessing Information Quality of a Community-Based Encyclopedia. In *Proceedings of the 2005 International Conference on Information Quality, ICIQ 2005*, pp. 442–454.

Sullivan, L.E. 1990. Circumscribing Knowledge: Encyclopedias in Historical Perspective. *The Journal of Religion* 70 (3): 315–339.

Sutton, F.X. 1962. Developing the Idea of a New Social Science Encyclopedia. *The American Behavioral Scientist* 6 (1): 27–30.

Tereszkiewicz, Anna. 2013. *Genre Analysis of Online Encyclopedias: The Case of Wikipedia*. Wydawnictwo UJ.

Todorović, M. 2018. From Diderot's *Encyclopedia* to Wales's Wikipedia: A Brief History of Collecting and Sharing Knowledge. *Journal KSIO* 1: 88–102.

Tropp, H. 1980. Capsule Reviews. *IEEE Annals of the History of Computing* 2 (1): 93.

Tucker, A.B. 2004. *Computer Science Handbook*, 2nd ed. Chapman & Hall.

Van Doren, C. 1962. The Idea of an Encyclopedia. *The American Behavioral Scientist* 6 (1): 23–26.

Wexelbaum, R.S. 2012. Is the Encyclopedia Dead? Evaluating the Usefulness of a Traditional Reference Resource. *Reference Reviews* 26 (7): 7–11.

Yeo, R. 1991. Reading Encyclopedias: Science and the Organization of Knowledge in British Dictionaries of Arts and Sciences, 1730–1850. *Isis* 82 (1): 24–49.

Yeo, R. 2001. *Encyclopaedic Visions: Scientific Dictionaries and Enlightenment Culture*. Cambridge University Press.

Yeo, R. 2007. Lost Encyclopedias: Before and After the Enlightenment. *Book History* 10 (1): 47–68.

MIX
Papier aus verantwortungsvollen Quellen
Paper from responsible sources
FSC® C105338

If you have any concerns about our products,
you can contact us on
ProductSafety@springernature.com

In case Publisher is established outside the EU,
the EU authorized representative is:
**Springer Nature Customer Service Center GmbH
Europaplatz 3, 69115 Heidelberg, Germany**

Printed by Libri Plureos GmbH
in Hamburg, Germany